THE LAW OF DEBT COLLECTION

2nd Edition

by
Margaret C. Jasper

Oceana's Legal Almanac Series
Law for the Layperson

2001
Oceana Publications, Inc.
Dobbs Ferry, New York

Information contained in this work has been obtained by Oceana Publications from sources believed to be reliable. However, neither the Publisher nor its authors guarantee the accuracy or completeness of any information published herein, and neither Oceana nor its authors shall be responsible for any errors, omissions or damages arising from the use of this information. This work is published with the understanding that Oceana and its authors are supplying information, but are not attempting to render legal or other professional services. If such services are required, the assistance of an appropriate professional should be sought.

Library of Congress Control Number: 2001135886

ISBN: 0-379-11358-9

Oceana's Legal Almanac Series: Law for the Layperson
ISSN 1075-7376

To My Husband Chris

Your love and support
are my motivation and inspiration

-and-

In memory of my son, Jimmy

Table of Contents

CHAPTER 3:
JUDGMENT ENFORCEMENT

CHAPTER 4:
DEBT COLLECTION BY TAXING AUTHORITIES

CHAPTER 5:
DEBT COLLECTION HARASSMENT

CHAPTER 6:
CREDIT REHABILITATION

CHAPTER 7:
IDENTITY THEFT

ABOUT THE AUTHOR

MARGARET C. JASPER is an attorney engaged in the general practice of law in South Salem, New York, concentrating in the areas of personal injury and entertainment law. Ms. Jasper holds a Juris Doctor degree from Pace University School of Law, White Plains, New York, is a member of the New York and Connecticut bars, and is certified to practice before the United States District Courts for the Southern and Eastern Districts of New York, the United States Court of Appeals for the Second Circuit, and the United States Supreme Court.

Ms. Jasper has been appointed to the panel of arbitrators of the American Arbitration Association and the law guardian panel for the Family Court of the State of New York, is a member of the Association of Trial Lawyers of America, and is a New York State licensed real estate broker and member of the Westchester County Board of Realtors, operating as Jasper Real Estate, in South Salem, New York. Margaret Jasper maintains a website at http://members.aol.com/JasperLaw.

Ms. Jasper is the author and general editor of the following legal almanacs: Juvenile Justice and Children's Law; Marriage and Divorce; Estate Planning; The Law of Contracts; The Law of Dispute Resolution; Law for the Small Business Owner; The Law of Personal Injury; Real Estate Law for the Homeowner and Broker; Everyday Legal Forms; Dictionary of Selected Legal Terms; The Law of Medical Malpractice; The Law of Product Liability; The Law of No-Fault Insurance; The Law of Immigration; The Law of Libel and Slander; The Law of Buying and Selling; Elder Law; The Right to Die; AIDS Law; The Law of Obscenity and Pornography; The Law of Child Custody; The Law of Debt Collection; Consumer Rights Law; Bankruptcy Law for the Individual Debtor; Victim's Rights Law; Animal Rights Law; Workers' Compensation Law; Employee Rights in the Workplace; Probate Law; Environmental Law; Labor Law; The Americans with Disabilities Act; The Law of Capital Punishment; Education Law; The Law of Violence Against Women; Landlord-Tenant Law; Insurance Law; Religion and the Law; Commercial Law; Motor Vehicle Law; Social Security Law; The Law of Drunk Driving; The Law of Speech and the First Amendment; Employment Discrimination Under Title VII; Hospital Liability Law; Home Mortgage Law Primer; Copyright Law; Patent Law; Trademark Law; Special Education Law; The Law of Attachment and Garnishment; Banks and their Customers; and Credit Cards and the Law.

INTRODUCTION

Consumer debt has reached an all time high, with credit card debt being a major factor. Individual bankruptcy filings have skyrocketed to a record number. Typically, an individual faced with a sudden crisis, such as illness, loss of employment, divorce, etc., finds their income reduced to the point where he or she is no longer able to pay their bills. Debts have to be prioritized, with rent or mortgage payments and utility bills of paramount concern. Meanwhile, the stack of credit card bills, loan payments, and automobile notes builds.

Debt collection is the process by which a creditor recovers money owed by individuals who are either unable or unwilling to pay their debts. When a due date passes with no recorded payment, the creditor's computer starts to churn out late notices, followed by telephone calls, and ultimately—if the amount is considerable—legal action to recover the debt. In the meantime, late fees and finance charges accrue, making it difficult for the debtor to catch up.

Many individuals become overwhelmed by this onslaught at a time when they are already vulnerable. Unethical creditors may prey on this vulnerability and try and recover debts by illegal means, such as using threatening language, misrepresenting the law, and using a variety of other pressure tactics. Thus, it is important that the debtor be aware of his or her rights and the laws designed to protect them should they find themselves in a financial bind.

This legal almanac explores the law of debt collection and is intended to help the debtor consider all of their available options. This almanac provides the debtor with an overview of the law applicable to debt collection, and what one may expect when debts go unpaid. There are laws which protect the debtor from harassment, threats and other illegal tactics used by those seeking to collect on a debt. This almanac also sets forth the types of debt and the manner in which different categories of debt are treated.

This almanac also offers advice to the debtor on ways to manage debt without having to resort to drastic measures, such as bankruptcy. Of course, the almanac does set forth scenarios where bankruptcy may be the preferred route once all other options have been considered. This almanac also discusses credit rehabilitation and cautions the consumer against unscrupulous businesses which claim to be able to "repair" bad credit.

In addition, this almanac discusses identity theft—a growing problem facing all consumers—and provides the reader with the information necessary to address this problem should they fall victim to this crime. Victims of identity theft are not only victimized by the criminal who misappropriated their identity, but are further victimized by the system when their credit rating is ruined through no fault of their own as they try to undo the damage caused by unauthorized procurement of credit in their name.

The Appendix sets forth statutes applicable to debt collection and provides other pertinent information and data. The Glossary contains definitions of many of the terms used throughout the almanac.

CHAPTER 1:
MANAGING DEBT

IN GENERAL

A debtor is one who owes a monetary debt to another, who is known as a creditor. Although being in debt may be unpleasant and embarrassing, the problem can be managed. The first step in effectively managing your debts is to examine your financial circumstances, as follows:

1. List all sources of monthly income, including such items as wages, pensions, social security, interest income, and child support.

2. List all of your necessary monthly expenses, including such items as food, clothing, housing, utilities, transportation costs, and medical expenses.

3. List all other monthly debts. Prioritize the debts according to their importance and overdue status.

4. Deduct the total necessary monthly expenses (Item #2) from the total monthly income (Item #1). If there is a balance left over, this would be the amount available to make payments on some of the other monthly debts (Item #3).

5. If there is not enough money left over to make all monthly payments, make payments according to the priorities set forth. For example, if the car payment is two months past due and subject to repossession, don't send a check to the "book of the month" club. In short, don't make payments on low priority bills, despite the pressure you may get from a collection agency.

6. If there is no money left over after paying the essentials, or if the debts are so overwhelming that it is unlikely they will ever be repaid in full, do not ignore the problem but consider your alternatives, as more fully discussed in this almanac.

TYPES OF DEBT

A debt is generally defined as an obligation or liability to pay. However, debts may be classified further according to certain factors, such as the type of lender and the rights the lender retained according to agreement, as set forth below.

Secured Debts

A debt is "secured" if the lender, by agreement, has retained some kind of interest in the borrower's property in return for making the loan. Secured debts usually involve large purchases, such as homes, automobiles, appliances and furniture. This security gives the lender some assurance that the debt will be repaid, or that the lender will not suffer a total loss if the borrower defaults. The secured item can be repossessed.

For example, when a home is purchased, the bank or mortgage company which finances the purchase retains the right to foreclose and sell the house if the payments are not made as agreed. The house is the security for the loan.

In addition, if an individual borrows money from a lending institution, such as a bank or finance company, the lender may require the borrower to pledge some item of value as collateral for the loan, such as a car. The loan is secured by the collateral, even though the collateral has nothing to do with the reason for borrowing the money.

A security interest also provides the secured party with the assurance that if the debtor files bankruptcy, the lender may be able to recover the value of the loan by taking possession of the collateral, instead of receiving only a fraction of the borrower's property after it is divided among all creditors, or nothing at all.

Automobile Repossession

As stated above, an exception to the requirement of obtaining a judgment also exists for automobile finance companies because the lender on an automobile loan generally retains a security interest in the car. Thus, it is legal for the lender to repossess an automobile when the debtor defaults on the payments. They commonly do so without notification.

The lender usually hires someone to track down the car and simply take it by whatever means possible, e.g. tow it, hot wire it, etc. That person is commonly referred to as the "repo man." He or she will use personal information, such as the debtor's home or workplace address, to find the car. If you are concerned that your car may be repossessed before you are able to catch up on your payments, don't leave it out in the open where it can easily be found. A garaged car is usually safe because the "repo" person is not legally permitted to break into your garage.

If, however, you find that your car has been repossessed, it is important to seek to reinstate the contract as soon as possible. The debtor can generally obtain the vehicle and reinstate the contract once all of the arrears, and any expenses incurred by the lender as a result of the repossession, are paid in full. The lender will usually try and sell the car if the debtor fails to reinstate the contract in a timely manner.

Depending on the law of the state in which you reside, the lender is generally required to give the debtor notice prior to the sale. If the contract is not reinstated within the time period required by law, the car will be sold. Unfortunately, the lender usually does not make an effort to sell the car for its retail value, therefore, you will still be liable for any deficiency between the sale price and the amount you still owe on the vehicle.

For example, if the balance on your car loan is $7,000, and the lender sells your car for $4,000, you will still be liable to the lender for the difference of $3,000 plus costs and legal fees.

The reader is advised to check the law of the state in which he or she lives on the specific rights afforded a consumer whose motor vehicle has been repossessed.

Unsecured Debts

Unsecured debts are those for which the lender has retained no interest in any of the items purchased. Thus, if the debtor defaults on the payments, the lender has no legal right to repossess any of the goods.

Unsecured debts are the most common, and may include: (i) credit card debt; (ii) medical expenses; and (iii) uncollateralized loans.

Joint Debts

Two or more people may incur joint debts. This situation may occur when an individual guarantees—i.e., co-signs—on another party's loan so that the borrower is approved. For example, a parent may co-sign for their child's automobile loan. If the original party defaults, the creditor will look to the co-signer for payments. Generally, the co-signer is as equally liable for the debt as the defaulting party.

Another scenario in which a third party may become obligated on another's loan is when the third party agrees, after the fact, to assume the original debtor's obligation. Again, both the original debtor and the party assuming the obligation are equally liable to the creditor for the debt.

A sample Agreement to Assume an Obligation is set forth at Appendix 1.

Spouses commonly incur joint debts. For example, a husband and wife may jointly apply for a credit card. If one spouse uses the credit line, and then defaults on the payments, the other spouse is still liable, whether or not he or she incurred the debt. Joint debts often raise problems following a divorce. For example, although the parties may agree that one spouse will pay the credit card payments, if he or she reneges, the other spouse is still liable for the debt. The innocent spouse's only recourse would be to sue the non-paying spouse for breach of the agreement. This can be expensive, time-consuming, and fruitless if the non-paying spouse is judgment proof.

DISCHARGING CONSUMER DEBT IN BANKRUPTCY

If the debtor's financial situation is so bad that there is no hope of getting out of debt, he or she may consider the option of filing bankruptcy. When faced with an imminent foreclosure sale, or wage garnishment, bankruptcy may provide the debtor with some breathing space. The filing of a bankruptcy action stays—i.e. suspends—any action being taken against the debtor.

Bankruptcy was provided by the federal government as a means for a debtor to get rid of a large number of his or her debts, so that they can begin a fresh start. These are known as "dischargeable" debts. However, once a debtor files bankruptcy, and the debts are discharged, he or she is precluded from doing so again for a period of approximately six years.

The bankruptcy court will generally review a statement of the debtor's financial condition and list of assets and liabilities. If it is determined that there are assets of value which are not statutorily exempt, the court may order those assets to be sold and the proceeds to be paid out to the creditors.

The debtor may be entitled to select exemptions available under the bankruptcy law or their own state's law, whichever provides the debtor with the maximum protection. The reader is advised to check the law of his or her jurisdiction.

There are, however, certain debts which are not dischargeable. These may include federal and state taxes, child support, student loans, and debts you failed to list in your filing papers, unless it is demonstrated that the creditor knew of your filing and failed to make a claim. Further, you would still be required to make payments on debts which are secured—e.g., an automobile loan—or return the secured property.

A more detailed discussion of bankruptcy laws and procedures may be found in this author's legal almanac entitled The Law of Bankruptcy for the Individual Debtor, also published by Oceana Publishing Company.

CHAPTER 2:
METHODS OF DEBT COLLECTION

IN GENERAL

If a consumer defaults on payments, the creditor will likely undertake some sort of debt collection. However, prior to being subjected to a formal lawsuit, one may wish to explore the possibility of an alternative method to resolve the dispute. If a debtor and creditor are unable to resolve the dispute in an informal manner, the creditor will likely attempt to recover the debt by suing the debtor in a court of law, particularly if the amount in dispute is significant.

A table of state statutes governing debt collection is set forth at Appendix 2.

INTERNAL DEBT COLLECTION DEPARTMENTS

The first attempts to collect a debt are usually nonjudicial, and undertaken by the internal collection department of the creditor. Initial contacts are made by letter or telephone. Absent success, some debt collectors take increasingly invasive measures to collect the debt. If the creditor is unable to collect the debt voluntarily from the debtor, the creditor's remedy is usually limited to litigation to acquire a judgment against the debtor.

The first contact the debtor may receive from a creditor is usually a form letter—a polite reminder about the past due account. If the debtor doesn't respond with payment, however, the letters continue, with language that gets stronger with each mailing. One should not take these letters personally because they are computer-generated, and the computer can't distinguish one debtor from the next.

A sample Creditor Demand Letter is set forth in the Appendix 3.

The debtor may also receive several phone calls. If the debtor intends to pay the bill, but is unable to do so due to financial constraints, a payment plan can be requested. In the early stages of collection, most creditors are willing to work within the debtor's budget. Make sure that the proposed plan is realistic. It's not going to do much good to enter into a payment agreement and default on it.

The creditor will usually request the debtor to confirm the payment agreement in writing. Generally, a letter setting forth the agreement will be sent to the debtor, requesting that the debtor sign and return the letter. This gives the creditor an advantage if the debtor defaults on the agreement as it provides a written acknowledgement of the debt.

A sample Payment Agreement Confirmation Letter is set forth in the Appendix 4.

Start off slowly, and propose small payments for a number of months, with increases at various intervals. For example, a debtor owes three hundred dollars on a revolving department store credit card. He or she offers to pay twenty dollars per month for the first three months, increasing to fifty dollars per month for the next three months, etc. In this way, the creditor can see that there is some prospect of recovery in the future.

The only problem with payment plans is that accrual of finance charges often defeats the plan. After a significant number of payments are made, one may find that the principal is the same—if not higher—than when the payments began. Ask the creditor to suspend the finance charges so all payments can be applied to reduce the principal. If so, the likelihood of success with the plan is increased. Some creditors will agree to waive the finance charges, others will absolutely refuse.

Companies usually establish a time period within which they try to collect a debt internally. If these efforts fail, and the creditor is unable to collect the debt or make a satisfactory payment agreement with the debtor, the creditor will generally place the account with an attorney or independent collection agency with whom the creditor contracts.

INDEPENDENT DEBT COLLECTION AGENCIES

Independent debt collection agencies generally earn a percentage of any amount they are able to collect. Thus, their business depends on getting money from you. Intimidation is central to their success. They are notorious for using threats, humiliation, misrepresentation, and other forms of harassment to get you to pay. It is important that you remain calm in response to these contacts and know your rights under the law.

As further discussed in this almanac, there are laws governing debt collection agency conduct with which they must comply or face legal consequences. For example, a debtor has the right to advise the collection agency that he or she no longer wishes to be contacted concerning collection of the debt. This notice should be in writing, and sent to the collection agency by certified mail with a return receipt requested. If the collection agency continues to make contact concerning collection, this is a violation, and they may be held liable for damages.

A sample Notice to Collection Agency to Cease Contact is attached at Appendix 5.

Do not give the collector what he or she wants, which is to scare you into handing over some money. Realize that there is little that they can do, despite the many threats one may read and hear. For example, one common tactic is to continually telephone the debtor. The purpose of these telephone calls is not only to demand payment, but to try and persuade the debtor to converse and give information that may be helpful in collection or in the enforcement of a judgment.

Some debt collectors request that the debtor provide them with post-dated checks even though the debtor states that their account does not presently have sufficient funds. The debt collector may assure the debtor that the check will not be processed without his or her consent. Don't fall for this routine. The debt collector often employs this tactic so that, if the check is dishonored, he or she can threaten the debtor with criminal bad check prosecution.

Although prosecution for bad checks is unlikely in this scenario, the mere threat can still be unsettling. It is wiser not to place oneself in this position in the first instance. In any event, under certain circumstances, using this tactic may expose the debt collector to liability for damages sustained by the debtor.

In this connection, the reader is advised to check the law of his or her own jurisdiction concerning the application and limitations of criminal bad check statutes.

The debt collector may also threaten immediate legal action to collect the debt. This is unlikely, particularly when they are dealing with a relatively small amount. The costs of litigation are high and often exceed the debt. Using a cost-benefit analysis, it is simply bad business to litigate every bad debt. When the amount is relatively small, most creditors will at some point simply take the loss—also known as a "charge off"—and satisfy themselves with ruining your credit rating.

Further, it is a violation for a debt collector to threaten legal action which is not intended to be taken. Also note that it is illegal for a collection agency to send you a form which appears to be a court document, such as a document resembling an official summons.

Another common tactic some collectors use is to tell the debtor that they are going to "take their home" or "garnishee their wages" if the debt is not paid within a certain amount of time. Despite what you are told by the collector—unless it pertains to taxes—they cannot immediately "take your home" or actually "collect" any money from you by way of attachment of your assets or wages, unless they acquire a judgment. As further set forth in Chapter 4, the requirement of obtaining a judgment does not apply to the taxing authorities, such as the Internal Revenue Service.

When you are subjected to abusive collection tactics, simply inform the collector that they are misrepresenting themselves, and that you know your rights. You can even spell it out for them in detail—recite the applicable law. Debt collectors dislike communicating with debtors who know their rights and can't be coerced. Ask the collector if you can tape the conversation for your records. This will likely intimidate the collector, and you may find that he or she actually hangs up on you.

The oppressive and abusive measures that debt collection agencies have been known to take has led to federal and state legislation designed to protect debtors. In addition, there exist a number of common-law theories under which an aggrieved debtor can retaliate against unfair debt collection procedures. Thus, it is important to be aware of your rights. If a collector violates your legal rights, you can sue and recover money for your damages. You may even be able to get the debt canceled. Your right to pursue legal action for debt collection harassment is further discussed in Chapter 5.

If you are faced with a particularly offensive collection agency, you may also want to notify the original creditor. Most times, the original creditor is unaware of the tactics used by the collection agency with which it contracts. Advise the original creditor that you plan to take legal action, and send a copy of the letter to the appropriate governmental agencies, as well as your attorney. You may gain some satisfaction in knowing that an abusive collection agency loses a client.

NONJUDICIAL DEBT COLLECTION

As discussed below, there are a number of methods by which a debtor can try and resolve a debt with the creditor before the creditor seeks to recover the debt by filing a formal legal action.

Compromise and Settlement

If you are concerned about protecting your credit rating, or want to avoid a lawsuit, you may consider compromising and settling the debt. The debt collector has an incentive to settle the matter, so that they can move on to other accounts, and receive their commission on your debt.

Creditors will usually consider accepting a reduced amount provided that amount is paid in full. If you have access to a lump sum of money, it may be worthwhile to offer the creditor an amount far below what is actually owed. For example, one may be able to reduce a three thousand dollar debt to fifteen hundred dollars—a fifty percent reduction—if they are able to come up with the lump sum of money.

As further discussed in chapter 6, there are agencies who advertise their ability to intervene on behalf of the debtor and work out agreements for repayment of the debt. However, if you are considering using such a service, it is crucial to fully investigate the background and reputation of such a company.

Even if the lawsuit has been filed, the parties can still settle the matter by entering into a stipulation. However, if the debtor defaults, the stipulation may provide that a judgment can be entered immediately upon default.

A sample Agreement to Compromise a Debt is set forth at Appendix 6.

Arbitration and Mediation

Another method of resolving a dispute without formal legal action is through arbitration or mediation. Many contracts provide for arbitration or mediation as the agreed methods to resolve a dispute. If there is no such prior agreement, the parties can also stipulate to arbitrate or mediate the dispute. The process is usually more economical and expedient than a trial. In an arbitration, the decision of the arbiter is binding on the parties. In a mediation, the mediator tries to assist the parties in reaching a mutually satisfying resolution, however, if the mediation is unsuccessful, the creditor is free to resort to more formal methods of debt recovery.

A more detailed discussion of arbitration and mediation may be found in this author's legal almanac entitled The Law of Dispute Resolution, also published by Oceana Publishing Company.

Confession of Judgment

A debt collector may ask the debtor to sign a confession of judgment in return for the cessation of all collection activities. A confession of judgment is an affidavit executed by the debtor which basically admits that the debtor owes the debt, and authorizes entry of a judgment in a certain sum. A confession of judgment gives the creditor the right to collect on the debt without requiring them to file a legal action to obtain a judgment. Signing a confession of judgment is not advisable, particularly if the debtor is looking to buy some time to satisfy the debt.

JUDICIAL DEBT COLLECTION

Most creditors will not pursue legal action to recover a relatively small debt, particularly if the projected costs of the action outweigh the recovery. However, if the debt is substantial enough to warrant a lawsuit, the creditor may seek to obtain a judgment to recover the debt.

Statute of Limitations

In order to take legal action to recover a debt, the legal action must be commenced within the applicable statute of limitations. A statute of limitations refers to the period within which an action must be commenced by law. Different types of actions carry different time periods. For example, some jurisdictions provide that a contract action must be commenced within six years, whereas a personal injury lawsuit must be commenced within three years. The reader is advised to check the laws of his or her jurisdiction concerning the applicable statute of limitations.

The Litigation Process

Litigation to recover a debt begins with the filing of a lawsuit. This is accomplished by service of a summons and complaint upon the debtor. Service is undertaken by a person authorized by law to serve legal documents, such as the sheriff or a process server. Many jurisdictions also permit a non-party, over the age of 18, to serve legal documents.

Depending on the jurisdiction, the party bringing the lawsuit is known as the plaintiff or petitioner, and the party against whom the lawsuit is filed is known as the defendant or respondent. The complaint details the plaintiff's claim against the defendant, and sets forth the legal theory under which the plaintiff seeks to prevail.

Upon receipt of the summons and complaint, the defendant must respond to the complaint within a prescribed period of time or risk losing the dispute by default. The defendant may serve an answer to the complaint, or may choose to make a motion seeking to dismiss the complaint prior to serving his or her answer. If the motion is granted, the case is dismissed. However, if the motion is denied, the defendant must serve an answer within a statutorily defined time period following the decision on the motion.

The defendant's answer admits or denies the allegations set forth in the complaint, and presents any defenses to the allegations that the defendant may have. Additionally, if the defendant has his or her own claims against the plaintiff, known as counterclaims, these allegations are also set forth in the defendant's answer. The plaintiff is then required to serve an answer addressing the counterclaim.

The litigation procedure, from initiation of the lawsuit to final disposition, is governed by the statutory law of the particular court in which the lawsuit is filed. During the pendency of the lawsuit, much of litigation is accomplished on paper. There are numerous motions which a party may file and ask the assigned judge to rule upon. A motion, which may be made orally or in writing, is an application to the court requesting an order or a ruling in favor of the applicant.

For example, a party may make a motion seeking some type of interim relief, such as the production of certain evidence. This may include, for example, proof that a debt is owed. The notice of motion and any supporting papers are served upon the other party, who usually responds in opposition to the motion.

Complex litigation usually involves a lengthy discovery process. Typical discovery may include the exchange of detailed information, the examination of documents and other evidence, and an oral examination of the parties and prospective witnesses in a proceeding known as a deposition or examination before trial.

During a deposition, the deponent is placed under oath, and must answer a series of questions asked by the parties or their attorneys. The sworn testimony given at the deposition is recorded by a legal stenographer, who prepares a transcript of the depositions for use at trial. The deposition testimony pins down each deponent's version of the facts, and can be used to impeach a party or non-party witness.

As the lawsuit nears trial, the judge will usually set the matter down for a settlement conference, in an attempt to resolve the dispute without going to trial. Absent a successful outcome, the lawsuit eventually goes to trial, after which a decision is rendered by the judge or jury. The parties may seek to appeal unfavorable decisions to higher courts. Once the appeals process has been exhausted, the decision is final and a prevailing plaintiff will be awarded an enforceable judgment.

As you can see, protracted litigation over a debt is in nobody's best interest. Legal fees for both the plaintiff and defendant could prove costly. It is unlikely that the defendant, who is already in debt, would be able to afford an attorney to handle the litigation. However, every individual has the right to represent themselves in a lawsuit. This is known as acting "pro se," and can be a creditor's nightmare. At this point, the creditor may be willing to take a reasonable offer below the debt amount. However, if you believe that you do not owe the debt, then by all means, you should try and fight it.

As set forth above, if you decide not to answer the complaint within the time required, you will be considered "in default." A default judgment will thereafter be awarded the plaintiff. Of course, this means that collection can begin in a relatively short period of time following commencement of the action. Judgment enforcement is discussed more fully in Chapter 3 of this almanac.

CHAPTER 3:
JUDGMENT ENFORCEMENT

IN GENERAL

If a creditor prevails in a legal action against the debtor for the amount owed, the court awards the creditor a "judgment" for money damages. The creditor is thereafter known as a judgment creditor and the defendant as the judgment debtor. If the judgment debtor does not voluntarily pay on the judgment amount, the plaintiff may attempt to "execute" on the judgment—i.e., recover the amount owed.

Once a creditor obtains a judgment, collecting a debt from an individual or business that is solvent is not as difficult because the judgment debtor purportedly has some interests to protect, e.g., a good credit rating. However, when the debtor is insolvent, or appears to be "judgment-proof"—i.e., has no discernable assets from which to collect the debt—or is simply reluctant to pay the debt, further debt collection techniques must be employed to recover the money owed the creditor.

THE JUDGMENT PROOF DEBTOR

A debtor who has no assets or wages that can be attached or garnished is often referred to as "judgment proof." For example, an elderly individual, who rents their living space, and survives on social security, without any assets except for those which would be deemed exempt, would be considered "judgment proof." An unemployed college student would also appear to be "judgment proof."

However, if it appears that the debtor's financial situation will change in the future—e.g., the college student will embark on a promising new career after graduation—depending on the jurisdiction, judgment creditors may patiently await the change in financial circumstances because they generally have a long time to enforce a judgment and collect the debt, e.g. ten or more years. Once that statutorily-prescribed time period ends, however, the debt is presumed satisfied unless the judgment debtor has acknowledged the debt or made a payment during that period. Either of these actions could renew and/or extend the time period for collection.

The reader is advised to check the law of his or her own jurisdiction concerning the time within which a debt must be recovered, and whether there are any rights to renew a judgment.

FINANCIAL DISCLOSURE

In order to determine whether the judgment debtor is solvent, the judgment creditor is entitled to inquire into the debtor's assets, and the debtor must comply. This information is obtained in a number of ways, depending on the jurisdiction and the court in which the judgment was awarded.

For example, the debtor or a third party, such as a bank, may be served with a subpoena requiring the debtor or other appropriate person to answer, under oath, a number of questions concerning the location and amount of the judgment debtor's assets. The subpoena may also call for the production of financial records. Failure to comply with the subpoena may result in a contempt proceeding and lead to court-ordered punishment for the offending party.

If the judgment creditor is able to uncover assets belonging to the judgment debtor, the judgment creditor may serve a restraining notice on the judgment debtor or a third party who is in possession of the judgment debtor's assets.

RESTRAINING NOTICE

A restraining notice instructs the judgment debtor, or a third party, that he or she cannot transfer or dispose of any assets of the judgment debtor. The restraining notice is not a levy or a lien on the assets, as further discussed below. It merely prevents their transfer until the judgment creditor acquires a levy or lien on the assets at which time the sheriff or other authorized law enforcement officer can execute and take the property.

Nevertheless, if the property which is the subject of the execution is "exempt," as further discussed below, the debtor can make a claim for exemption and the sheriff would be prevented from seizing the exempt property.

METHODS OF JUDGMENT ENFORCEMENT

In General

Whether a judgment is awarded as a result of a litigated dispute, a confession of judgment, or a default, the collection procedures are the same. There are a number of methods by which a creditor may enforce a judgment and recover a debt from a debtor. For example, the creditor may seize money from a debtor's bank account, attach the debtor's business income or garnish a portion of a debtor's wages. The creditor may also be able to seize personal or real property owned by the debtor, or money owed to the debtor by third parties.

If a creditor creates a lien on the real property of the debtor, the creditor will generally get paid when the property is sold or refinanced. The lien may arise by agreement, statute, or through litigation between the parties. The proceeds from the sale of the debtor's property are used to satisfy the debt to the creditor.

In some states, a lien is automatically created when the court enters its judgment. In others, you must file a document to create a lien. Although recovering a debt by creating a lien may take a long time, it requires little effort on the part of the creditor, who merely waits for the sale or refinance to occur. In addition, every state authorizes a creditor to collect interest on a debt—generally at a statutory rate—while waiting to get paid.

Attachment and Garnishment

Attachment and garnishment are the two most common remedies available to a creditor to recover money owed by the debtor. Attachment is a limited statutory remedy whereby a creditor has the property of a debtor seized to satisfy the debt. The process of "attachment and execution" permits a creditor, with the assistance of the sheriff or marshall, to take or "seize" the debtor's personal property—such as a car—and then sell it. Thus, attachment refers to taking legal possession of the debtor's property and execution refers to the sale of the attached property to satisfy the debt.

Garnishment refers to the process of taking something belonging to the debtor which is being held by a third party, known as the "garnishee." For example, if a creditor "garnishes" a debtor's bank account, the bank is the "garnishee" because the bank is holding the funds in the debtor's account.

The remedies of attachment and garnishment are similar in many respects. Both are statutory remedies, and Federal courts follow state rules as to the availability of one or both remedies. In many states, the terms attachment and garnishment are used interchangeably and, in fact, garnishment is often referred to as a form of attachment. In some states, garnishment is not a separate remedy but rather a proceeding ancillary to attachment, while in other states, garnishment is an independent remedy.

The primary difference between attachment and garnishment is that attachment is directed to property in the possession of the debtor, whereas garnishment is directed to the property of the debtor that is being held by the garnishee. Attached property is seized pending execution whereas garnished property is generally left in the care and custody of the garnishee until surrendered to the creditor.

Thus, through attachment and garnishment, a creditor collects, applies or subjects personal property, real property, wages or funds owned by or due to a debtor, to the debt owed to the creditor. Any claim, which is due from one person to another whether arising from a personal loan, installment purchase, tort action, contract action or any other action can be satisfied in whole or part by the use of attachment or garnishment proceedings.

Wage Garnishment

For example, a creditor may "garnish" a debtor's wages to satisfy the debt. Depending on the jurisdiction, the judgment creditor is entitled to a statutorily prescribed percentage of the debtor's net pay. Generally, the sheriff will serve the employer with a wage garnishment. The employer must then deduct the statutory amount from the debtor's paycheck and forward it to the sheriff. The sheriff deducts their fees, and sends the balance to the judgment creditor.

The federal government has limited wage garnishment so that no amount may be withheld for any week unless the debtor's disposable earnings exceed thirty times the federal minimum hourly wage as prescribed in the Fair Labor Standard Act in effect at the time the earnings are payable.

Bank Execution

The judgment creditor may also make an application to the court for an execution on the bank account of the judgment debtor. The bank execution gives the judgment creditor permission to allow the sheriff to seize the proceeds of the account of the judgment debtor.

Following issuance of the bank execution, the sheriff will generally serve the execution on judgment debtor's bank. The bank generally must notify the judgment debtor of the execution. After a prescribed period of time,—e.g., 15 days—if the judgment debtor does not claim an exemption, the bank must turn the funds over to the sheriff, who deducts their fees, and sends the balance to the judgment creditor.

The judgment debtor has the right to petition the court if he or she believes that the money in the bank account is exempt. For example, the funds may be social security or unemployment compensation income, which is exempt.

Property Execution

A property execution is usually delivered to the sheriff, or other designated enforcement officer, so that he or she can enforce it. The sheriff will then demand payment and place a levy on the judgment debtor's assets. The type, amount and whereabouts of the debtor's assets should be specified and included with a copy of the execution sent to the sheriff.

The sheriff is obligated to levy any property specifically identified by the creditor so as to avoid dissipation of the assets. The manner in which a levy takes place generally involves delivery of the property execution to the custodian of the property, inspection and inventory of the property, and may also involve the physical relocation of the property. Property subject to execution may be sold at a public auction.

Real Property Execution

A judgment creditor may also file a lien against the debtor's home. However, unless the debt is significant, it is not usual for the creditor to proceed with a foreclosure and sale of the home to recover the debt, as this is a costly undertaking. Nevertheless, the mere filing of a lien against one's home is often enough to get a debtor to negotiate a settlement. In any event, the debtor is prevented from refinancing or selling the home until the lien is satisfied.

Homestead Exemption

Some states provide the debtor with a certain level of protection under a law generally known as a "homestead exemption." Depending on the jurisdiction, this may completely protect the debtor's home from a foreclosure sale, or at the very least, may provide the debtor with the exemption amount if the home is sold to satisfy the debt. Again, however, if the collector is a taxing authority, a homestead exemption may not be applicable. Further, if the debtor defaults on his or her mortgage, the lender can foreclose on the property and force a sale.

Depending on the jurisdiction, the law may provide a redemption period following a forced sale of the debtor's home. During this period of time, the debtor may be able to regain ownership to the property by paying off the debt, as well as court costs and other expenses. The reader is advised to check the applicable redemption laws of his or her jurisdiction.

Construction Lien

A construction lien—also referred to as a mechanic's lien—is a claim created by law which allows for a lien to be placed against the real property of the debtor for the purpose of securing a priority of payment of the price of work performed and materials furnished.

Statutory Exemptions

In order to afford some degree of protection to the debtor, each state has designated certain items which are exempt from execution. The homestead exemption is discussed above. Other exempt items may include an automobile, retirement pension, social security income, clothing and personal items. The reader is advised to check the law of his or her own jurisdiction to determine the applicable exemptions, and the procedure to follow to claim the exemption.

Satisfaction of Judgment and Release of Lien

When a judgment is paid, a satisfaction of judgment and release of lien, if applicable, must be filed with the proper authorities within a certain time period after the payment is made. A copy of the satisfaction of judgment is usually required to be sent to the judgment debtor. If the judgment is paid, in part, a partial satisfaction of judgment may be filed.

A sample satisfaction of judgment and release of lien is set forth at Appendix 7.

WRONGFUL ATTACHMENT OR GARNISHMENT

Although many precautions are taken by the courts in issuing attachment or garnishment orders, there are times when the order is improperly or fraudulently obtained. In these cases, the debtor has some options to pursue to obtain compensation for his or her damages, as set forth below.

Malicious Prosecution Action

A malicious prosecution action requires the debtor to show that he or she was the successful party in an action which determined the validity of the attachment. Further, the debtor must usually show that the attachment was brought by the creditor maliciously, without probable cause. The debtor must further show that he or she was damaged in some respect. Most states require a wrongful sequestration of property or the arrest of the person before the court will entertain a malicious prosecution suit. Even if the creditor eventually wins in the primary suit against the debtor, the attachment may still be wrongful if adequate grounds did not exist. Each state has its own requirements for malicious prosecution suits. Some states require a showing of malice on the part of the creditor while other states require a showing of a lack of probable cause.

Liability on the Attachment or Garnishment Bond

Another remedy for wrongful attachment is for the debtor to sue on the attachment or garnishment bond, if one was required. Most states generally require that before an attachment or garnishment shall issue, the plaintiff creditor must post a bond conditioned to pay the costs and damages which the defendant debtor may sustain if the order was wrongfully issued. The right to bring an action on such a bond depends upon the obligations specifically set forth in the bond.

Abuse of Process Actions

The abuse of process action is generally brought where there has been an excessive garnishment or attachment—i.e., where the creditor has attached more of the debtor's property or obtained a greater garnishment against him than was necessary to secure the debt owed.

Damages

The statutes of each state determine the type and extent of damages recoverable in an action for wrongful attachment or garnishment. Normally, the defendant can recover all the actual damages which he sustained as a natural result of the wrongful attachment or garnishment. Unusual, remote or speculative damages are not recoverable.

Compensatory Damages

Compensatory damages are those damages which attempt to place the debtor back in the position he was in prior to the wrongful act. If property has been lost or destroyed, the debtor may recover the value of the property at the time it was seized. If the goods were damaged, the debtor may recover the value prior to the damage. Damages caused by a detention of the property may be recoverable as well as the loss of profits or injury to his business, the loss due to depreciation in value of the property, loss of use of the property, and the loss of interest. Damages for mental suffering may also be recoverable if caused by the wrongful garnishment or attachment. Many states permit the debtor to recover the cost of attorney's fees and court costs.

Punitive Damages

The debtor may also be entitled to punitive damages. Punitive damages are those damages awarded as a punishment against the wrongdoer, and are supposed to act as a deterrent against further wrongdoing. Punitive damages are usually awarded in actions where the attachment or garnishment, in addition to being wrongful, was also done maliciously, willfully and without probable cause. In other words, the attachment was issued for the purpose of harassing or oppressing the debtor, rather than to preserve legal rights. For example, punitive damages have been awarded in suits where there was an attachment of exempt property with knowledge of the exemption or where false grounds were alleged.

SECURED TRANSACTIONS UNDER ARTICLE 9 OF THE UNIFORM COMMERCIAL CODE (U.C.C.)

UCC Article 9 governs *secured* transactions. Because a security agreement is also a contract, it must comply with any other state laws governing contracts. Thus, the reader is advised to further check the law of his or her own jurisdiction when researching a specific issue.

Article 9 applies to any transaction which is intended to create a security interest in personal property or fixtures, including goods, documents, instruments, general intangibles, chattel paper or accounts; and to sales of chattel paper or accounts. Article 9 also applies to security interests created by contract, as set forth in the statute. The purpose of Article 9 is to include all *consensual* security interests in personal property and fixtures under one Article.

Exclusions from Article 9 include but are not limited to landlord's liens, transfers of employee wage claims; governmental transfers; transfers of insurance claims; transfers of real estate liens or leases; and transfers of tort claims. In addition, statutory liens are not governed by Article 9, but by the individual statute that creates them. Statutory liens may take priority over a perfected security interest unless the statute provides otherwise.

Unless the secured party is in possession of the collateral pursuant to agreement—i.e., the collateral is "pledged"—a security interest is not enforceable against the debtor or third parties, and cannot attach until the debtor has signed a security agreement. The agreement to provide for a security interest must be in writing, signed by the debtor, and must describe the collateral.

The requirement of a writing is for evidentiary purposes in case a future conflict arises over the terms of the agreement and the identity of the collateral. Therefore, if the collateral is pledged, the need for a writing is of less importance and thus not required by the statute. Additional terms in a security agreement may include the amount of the debt and terms of repayment; and risk of loss and insurance provisions.

Value must be given in return for the security interest in order for it to attach. Value refers to any consideration sufficient to support a simple contract. For example: Buyer purchases a washing machine from Seller on an installment basis. Buyer and Seller agree that Seller will retain a security interest in the washing machine in case Buyer reneges on the payments. The sale of the washing machine to Buyer is the consideration which supports the contract.

A security interest cannot attach until the debtor has rights in the collateral. A pledged security agreement exists when the debtor transfers the collateral to the secured party in exchange for a loan. An example of a pledged security agreement would be where an individual leaves an item with a pawnbroker in return for a cash payment and the right to redeem the item.

The "perfection" of a security agreement allows a secured party to gain priority to the collateral over any third party. In general, the secured party is protected against any subsequent creditors and transferees of the debtor. In addition, the secured party's interest is superior to those of unsecured creditors in bankruptcy proceedings instituted by or against the debtor.

To perfect a security agreement, the filing of a financing statement is generally required unless an exception exists, as set forth in the statute. The purpose of the filing is to give public notice of the security interest. In general, most financing statements, other than those regarding land-related collateral, must be filed with the register of deeds in the county of the debtor's residence.

The financing statement generally must contain:

1. The names and addresses of the debtor and the secured party;

2. A description of the collateral; and

3. The signature of the debtor.

However, if the security agreement itself contains the above information, its filing may be sufficient to comply with this section.

Again, an exception to the filing requirement exists if the secured party takes possession of the security interest. If filing or possession takes place prior to attachment, the security interest is perfected at the time the requirements of attachment are met as set forth above

If the secured party assigns a perfected security interest to another, the perfected status of the security interest against creditors of the original debtor remains intact, and no further filing is required.

Article 9 defines *collateral* as property subject to a security interest, including accounts and chattel paper. Chattel paper refers to a writing which evidences both a monetary obligation and a security interest in goods. The collateral may remain in the possession of the debtor, or may be placed in the possession of the secured party, while the debt remains unpaid.

If the secured party is in possession of the collateral, he is required to use reasonable care in preserving the collateral. However, the obligation to pay reasonable expenses are chargeable to the debtor, and also secured by the collateral. A type of such expense is insurance coverage. Thus, the risk of accidental loss or damage to the collateral is borne by the debtor if there is insufficient insurance coverage.

The secured party is entitled to hold any increase or profits received from the collateral as additional security, other than money. If the collateral generates any money, the secured party must turn it over to the debtor, or apply it to reduce the secured obligation. Collateral may be repledged by the secured party provided it does not impair the debtor's right to redeem the collateral.

If the secured party fails to meet the obligations imposed under the statute, he is liable for any resulting loss. However, the secured party does not thereby lose his security interest.

If the secured party is aware that collateral is owned by a non-debtor, the owner is not liable for the debt. In addition, the owner has the same right as the debtor to: (i) receive a statement of account; (ii) receive notice of and make objections to a secured party's proposal to retain the collateral to satisfy the debt; (iii) redeem the collateral; (iv) obtain injunctive relief; and (v) recover losses caused by the secured party's actions or inactions.

A secured party may release all or a part of any collateral described in a filed financing statement by signing a statement of release. The statement of release must contain: (i) a description of the collateral being released; (ii) the names and addresses of the debtor and secured party; and (iii) the financing statement file number.

Whether a debtor is in default depends on the terms of the security agreement. For example, an agreement will invariably provide that failure to make payments required under the agreement constitutes default.

In addition to any rights and remedies provided in the security agreement in case of default, Article 9 affords the secured party further relief. For example, the secured party may execute against—i.e., reduce the claim to judgment and request the sheriff to levy—the debtor's property, which is then sold and the proceeds applied to the debt. If the agreement covers both real and personal property, he may foreclose on the real property.

In addition, the secured party may take possession of the collateral, if it is not already in his possession, or may sell the collateral and apply the proceeds of the sale to satisfy the claim. Of course, if there is any deficiency after sale—an amount still owing after the sale proceeds have been applied to the debt—the debtor is still liable for the deficiency, unless the underlying transaction is a sale of accounts or chattel paper and the security agreement provides for a deficiency judgment.

At any time before the secured party has disposed of the collateral, the debtor—or another secured party—may redeem the collateral by fulfilling the obligations secured by the collateral, as well as reimbursing the secured party for any expenses reasonably incurred in connection with the debtor's default. This may include legal fees and costs.

If a secured party proposes to retain the collateral in full satisfaction of the obligation, written notice of the proposal must be sent to the debtor absent the debtor's prior renunciation of the collateral. If the debtor fails to object, the secured party may retain the collateral.

Unless the collateral is perishable or subject to a rapid decline in value, the debtor is entitled to reasonable notice of the time and place of any public sale, or of the time after which any private sale is to be made.

If the security agreement secures an indebtedness, the secured party must account to the debtor for any surplus proceeds resulting from a sale of the collateral. However, if the underlying transaction is a sale of accounts or chattel paper, the debtor is only entitled to an accounting and surplus if the agreement provides for it.

CHAPTER 4:
DEBT COLLECTION BY TAXING AUTHORITIES

IN GENERAL

State and Federal Income Taxes

Taxing authorities are not required to file a legal action to obtain a judgment in order to collect taxes owed. The federal and state taxing authorities are entitled to collect taxes you owe on your tax return but fail to pay. The first contact you get from the taxing authority will generally be a bill or notice of assessment telling you how much you owe. If they do not receive a payment or request for a payment plan, the next step is usually a final notice. Again, if there is no response, collection action may begin shortly thereafter.

The debtor may be able to work out a payment plan for payment of their federal or state taxes, however, interest and penalties will continue to accrue. In order to have a payment plan approved, the debtor is generally required to complete a financial disclosure form. In the meantime, the taxing authority may stop collection action, but will likely file a lien against the debtor to protect their interests.

Property Taxes

Homeowners are responsible for taxes which are based on the value of their property. Such taxes may include school taxes and municipal taxes, collectively referred to as property taxes. If you do not pay your property taxes within a prescribed period of time, the local taxing authority may be entitled to sell your property in a tax sale to recover the amount owed. Following such a sale, there may be a redemption period available to the debtor to regain his or her property. The reader is again advised to check the law of his or her own jurisdiction to ascertain their rights under the applicable law.

INTERNAL REVENUE SERVICE TAX COLLECTION

In General

After a taxpayer's federal tax return is filed, the tax return is checked for mathematical accuracy, and the tax due is compared to all amounts paid. If there is any money owed, the taxpayer will be sent a bill. The issuance of the tax bill begins the tax collection process. The first bill sent explains the reason for the balance due and demands payment in full. It will include the tax due plus penalties and interest that are added to the unpaid balance from the date the taxes were due. The calculation of interest and penalties are further discussed below.

The taxpayer should not ignore the bill but must either pay the tax due in full or make payment arrangements to satisfy their tax obligation, as discussed below. To ensure that the payment is properly credited to the taxpayer's account, the taxpayer should make their check or money order payable to the United States Treasury and notate the primary social security number or employer identification number, the tax year and form number, and their telephone number on their check or money order.

If the taxpayer believes the tax bill is inaccurate, they should contact the IRS office that sent the bill, by mail or telephone, or visit their nearest IRS office. The taxpayer should mail or bring a copy of the bill and copies of any records such as, the front and back of canceled checks or money orders, or other information that will help the IRS determine whether a mistake has been made. If you are communicating with the IRS by mail, it is important that you do not send original documents. You may also contact the IRS by telephone to discuss the bill. The IRS may be reached by calling 1-800-829-1040.

If the bill is correct, but the taxpayer cannot pay the full amount due, they should pay as much as possible and immediately call the IRS to discuss payment of the remaining balance, as further discussed below.

The IRS has considerable rights under the law which are generally not available to other debt collectors. For example, they can share your tax information with city and state tax agencies, and can also contact third parties, such as neighbors, banks, and employers to investigate the case. If the taxpayer ignores the bill and/or refuses to pay their tax or make payment arrangements, the IRS may take enforced collection action, which could include

1. Filing a Notice of Federal Tax Lien,

2. Serving a Notice of Levy; or

3. Offset of any refund due the taxpayer.

Federal Tax Lien

A federal tax lien gives the IRS legal claim to the taxpayer's property as security or payment for the outstanding tax liability. A federal tax lien attaches to all of the taxpayer's property, such as their house and car, and all their rights to property, such as their bank accounts. The law requires the IRS to notify the taxpayer, in writing, within 5 business days after the filing of a lien. Notice may given in person, left at the taxpayer's home or usual place of business, or sent by certified or registered mail to the taxpayer's last known address. By filing a Notice of Federal Tax Lien, the Government provides public notice to the taxpayer's creditors that the government has a claim against the taxpayer's property, including property that was acquired after the lien was filed. Once a lien is filed, it may harm the taxpayer's credit rating.

However, a Notice of Federal Tax Lien cannot be filed until:

1. The IRS assesses the taxpayer's liability;

2. The IRS sends the taxpayer a Notice and Demand for Payment—the bill that tells the taxpayer how much they owe in taxes; and

3. The taxpayer neglects or refuses to fully pay the debt within 10 days after the IRS notifies them about it.

When the tax is paid in full, along with any interest, penalties and lien recording fees, the IRS will issue a document known as a "Release of Notice of Federal Tax Lien" which may be filed as evidence that the tax lien has been satisfied. The release will generally be issued within 30 days after the taxpayer satisfies the tax liability. If the taxpayer submits a bond to the IRS that guarantees payment of the tax liability, the IRS will release the lien within 30 days after they accept the bond. In general, a tax lien releases automatically after the expiration of 10 years from the date the tax was assessed if the IRS has not refiled the lien.

If the IRS does not release a Notice of Federal Tax Lien when it should be released, the taxpayer may sue the federal government for damages. In addition, by law, a filed notice of tax lien can be withdrawn if:

1. The notice was filed too soon or not according to IRS procedures;

2. The taxpayer entered into an installment agreement to pay the debt on the notice of lien (unless the agreement provides otherwise);

3. Withdrawal will speed collecting the tax; or

4. Withdrawal would be in the taxpayer's best interest as determined by the Taxpayer Advocate, and in the best interest of the government.

The taxpayer may file an appeal within 30 days of the date they are given notice that the tax lien has been filed. Some valid bases for appeal include:

1. The taxpayer paid all the taxes owed before the IRS filed the lien;

2. The IRS assessed the tax and filed the lien when the taxpayer was in bankruptcy and subject to the automatic stay available during bankruptcy;

3. The IRS made a procedural error in an assessment;

4. The time to collect the tax—called the statute of limitations—expired before the IRS filed the lien;

5. The taxpayer did not have an opportunity to dispute the assessed liability;

6. The taxpayer wishes to discuss the collection options; or

7. The taxpayer wishes to make spousal defenses, e.g., an innocent spouse claim where the taxes were owed by one spouse but assessed against both because a joint return was filed.

At the conclusion of the appeal, the IRS Office of Appeals will issue a determination. That determination may support the continued existence of the filed federal tax lien or it may determine that the lien should be released or withdrawn. The taxpayer will have a 30-day period, starting with the date of the determination, to bring a suit to contest the determination in Tax Court.

Federal Tax Levy

A levy is another method the IRS may use to collect taxes that are not paid voluntarily. A levy is a legal seizure of the taxpayer's property to satisfy a tax debt. Levies are different from liens. A lien is a claim used as security for the tax debt whereas a levy actually takes the property to satisfy the tax debt. A levy means that the IRS, by legal authority, may take and sell the taxpayer's property to satisfy a tax debt. Levies can be made on property that the taxpayer holds, such as their car, boat, or house, or on property that belongs to the taxpayer but is held by a third party, such as wages held by an employer or funds on deposit at a bank.

The IRS usually levies only after these three requirements are met:

1. The IRS assessed the tax and sent the taxpayer a Notice and Demand for Payment;

2. The taxpayer neglected or refused to pay the tax; and

3. The IRS sent the taxpayer a Final Notice of Intent to Levy and a Notice of Right to Hearing at least 30 days before the levy.

As with a lien, notice may be given in person, left at the taxpayer's home or usual place of business, or sent to the taxpayer's last known address by certified mail, return receipt requested.

The taxpayer may file an appeal with the IRS Office of Appeals within 30 days of the date of the Final Notice of Intent to Levy and Notice of Right to Hearing. Some valid bases for appeal include:

1. The taxpayer paid all taxes owed before the IRS sent the levy notice;

2. The IRS assessed the tax and sent the levy notice when the taxpayer was in bankruptcy and subject to the automatic stay available during bankruptcy;

3. The IRS made a procedural error in an assessment;

4. The time to collect the tax expired before the IRS sent the levy notice;

5. The taxpayer did not have an opportunity to dispute the assessed liability;

6. The taxpayer wishes to discuss the collection options; or

7. The taxpayer wishes to make spousal defenses, as set forth above.

As with a lien, at the conclusion of the appeal, the IRS Office of Appeals will issue a determination. That determination may support the levy action or it may determine that the levy should be released. The taxpayer will have a 30-day period, starting with the date of determination, to bring a suit to contest the determination in Tax Court.

If the IRS levies the taxpayer's salary or wages, the levy will end when:

1. The levy is released;

2. The taxpayer pays the tax debt; or

3. The time expires for legally collecting the tax.

If the IRS levies the taxpayer's bank account, the bank is required to hold funds up to the amount of the tax liability for 21 days during which time the taxpayer may try and resolve any problems from the levy or make other payment arrangements. After the 21 day period expires, the bank must send the money being held, plus any applicable interest, to the IRS.

If the IRS makes a mistake in levying the taxpayer's bank account, the taxpayer may file a claim for reimbursement. In addition, if the taxpayer paid bank charges because of a mistake made, the taxpayer may be entitled to a reimbursement. To be reimbursed, the taxpayer must file a claim with the IRS within 1 year after their bank charged the fee.

The IRS must release the levy if any of the following occur:

1. The taxpayer pays the tax, penalty, and interest owed;

2. The IRS discovers that the time for collection ended before the levy was served;

3. The taxpayer provides documentation proving that releasing the levy will help the IRS collect the tax;

4. The taxpayer has, or is about to enter into, an approved, current installment agreement, unless the agreement says the levy does not have to be released;

5. The IRS determines that the levy is creating a significant economic hardship for the taxpayer.

6. The expense of selling the property would be more than the tax debt.

The IRS may release the taxpayer's levied property prior to the sale date if:

1. The taxpayer pays the amount of the government 's interest in the property;

2. The taxpayer enters into an escrow arrangement;

3. The taxpayer furnishes an acceptable bond;

4. The taxpayer makes an acceptable agreement for paying the tax; or

5. The expense of selling the taxpayer's property would be more than the tax debt.

By law, some property cannot be levied or seized including:

1. School books and certain clothing;

2. Fuel, provisions, furniture, and personal effects for a household, totaling $6,250;

3. Books and tools used in the taxpayer's trade, business, or profession, totaling $3,125;

4. Unemployment benefits;

5. Undelivered mail;

6. Certain annuity and pension benefits;

7. Certain service-connected disability payments;

8. Workmen's compensation benefits;

9. Salary, wages, or income included in a judgment for court-ordered child support payments;

10. Certain public assistance payments;

11. A minimum weekly exemption for wages, salary, and other income.

The IRS may return levied property under certain circumstances, including:

1. If the IRS levies before they send the taxpayer two required notices;

2. If the IRS levies before the taxpayer's time for responding to the notices has passed—10 days for the Notice and Demand and 30 days for the Notice of Intent to Levy and the Notice of Right to Hearing;

3. If it was determined that the IRS did not follow their own procedures;

4. If the IRS agrees to let the taxpayer pay in installments;

5. Returning the property will help the taxpayer pay their taxes;

6. Returning the property is in the taxpayer's best interest and the government's best interest.

After the taxpayer's property is seized, the IRS must usually wait 60 days before they can sell it. The IRS will post a public notice of a pending sale, usually in local newspapers or flyers and deliver the original notice of sale to the taxpayer or send it to the taxpayer by certified mail.

After placing the notice, the IRS must wait at least 10 days before conducting the sale, unless the property is perishable and must be sold immediately. Before the sale, the IRS will compute a minimum bid price. This bid is usually 80% or more of the forced sale value of the property, after subtracting any liens. If the taxpayer disagrees with the minimum bid price, they can appeal it.

The taxpayer may also ask that the IRS sell the seized property within 60 days. The IRS will grant the taxpayer's request unless it is in the government's best interest to keep the property.

After the sale, the IRS first uses the proceeds to pay the expenses of the levy and sale. Then they use any remaining amount to pay the tax bill. If the proceeds of the sale are less than the total of the tax bill and the expenses of levy and sale, the taxpayer will still have to pay the unpaid tax.

If the proceeds of the sale are more than the total of the tax bill and the expenses of the levy and sale, the IRS will notify the taxpayer about the surplus money and will advise them on how to go about obtaining a refund. However, if someone, such as a mortgagee or other lienholder, makes a claim that is superior to that of the taxpayer, the IRS will pay that claim before they refund any money to the taxpayer.

The taxpayer or anyone with an interest in the property may redeem the real estate within 180 days after the sale by paying the purchaser the amount paid for the property, plus interest at 20% annually.

Interest and Penalties

The IRS charges interest, compounded daily, on any unpaid tax from the due date of the return until the date of payment. The interest rate is the federal short-term rate plus 3 percent. That rate is determined every three months. In addition, if the taxpayer files on time but doesn't pay on time, they will generally have to pay a late payment penalty of one-half of one percent of the tax owed for each month, or part of a month, that the tax remains unpaid after the due date, up to 25 percent. The one-half of one percent rate increases to one percent if the tax remains unpaid after several bills have been sent out and the IRS issues a notice of intent to levy.

If the taxpayer does not file on time and owes tax, they may owe an additional penalty for failure to file unless they can show reasonable cause for filing untimely. The combined penalty is 5 percent—4.5% late filing, 0.5% late payment—for each month, or part of a month, that the return was late, up to 25%. The late filing penalty applies to both the tax shown on the return and any additional tax found to be due, as reduced by any credits for withholding and estimated tax and any timely payments made with the return. After five months, if the taxpayer still has not paid the tax owed, the 0.5% failure-to-pay penalty continues to run, up to 25%, until the tax is paid. Thus, the total penalty for failure to file and pay can be 47.5%—22.5% late filing, 25% late payment—of the tax owed. Also, if the return was over 60 days late, the minimum failure-to-file penalty is the smaller of $100 or 100% of the tax required to be shown on the return.

The penalties for filing late and paying late may be waived if the taxpayer has reasonable cause for being late. If the taxpayer believes they have reasonable cause for being late, they should contact the IRS and provide them with their explanation. Generally, interest charges may not be waived and continue to accrue until all assessed tax, penalties, and interest are paid in full.

Installment Agreements

The taxpayer should file their return on time even if they cannot pay all of the amount owed. By filing on time, the late filing penalty is avoided. One should endeavor to pay as much of the amount owed as possible in order to reduce the amount of interest and late payment penalties assessed. If the taxpayer cannot pay the full amount due as shown on their tax return, they may ask to make monthly installment payments. However, the taxpayer will be charged interest and may be charged a late payment penalty unless they can show reasonable cause for not paying their tax due by April 15, even if their request to pay in installments is granted.

As of January 1, 2000, if the taxpayer filed a timely return and is paying their tax pursuant to an installment agreement, the penalty is one-quarter of one percent for each month, or part of a month, that the installment remains unpaid. Thus, the taxpayer is advised to see whether they can obtain alternate and less costly financing to pay their taxes before requesting an installment agreement. For example, the interest rate a bank charges may be lower than the combination of interest and penalties imposed by the Internal Revenue Code.

Even though the IRS may give the taxpayer an installment agreement, they may still file a Notice of Federal Tax Lien to secure the government's interest until the taxpayer makes the final payment. However, they cannot levy against the taxpayer's property (i) while the request for an installment agreement is being considered; (ii) while the agreement is in effect; (iii) for 30 days after the request for an agreement has been rejected; or (iv) for any period while an appeal of the rejection is being evaluated by the IRS.

A sample IRS Installment Agreement Request Form is set forth at Appendix 8.

OFFER IN COMPROMISE

A taxpayer may qualify for an Offer in Compromise if they are unable to pay their taxes in full or if they are facing severe or unusual economic hardship. The purpose of an Offer in Compromise is to settle a taxpayer's liability for less than the full amount owed. The ultimate goal is a resolution that is in both the government's and the taxpayer's best interest.

The IRS may legally compromise a tax liability for one of the following reasons:

1. Doubt as to Liability—There is doubt as to whether or not the assessed tax is correct;

2. Doubt as to Collectibility—There is doubt that the taxpayer could ever pay the full amount of the tax owed. However, the total amount owed must be greater than the sum of the taxpayer's assets and future income.

3. Promotion of Effective Tax Administration—There is no doubt that the assessed tax is correct and no doubt that the amount owed could be collected, but the taxpayer has an economic hardship or other special circumstances which may allow the IRS to accept less than the total balance due.

In determining an amount to offer in compromise of one's tax liability, the taxpayer should offer an amount that is equal to or exceeds the taxpayer's equity in assets, their ability to make installment payments from future income, amounts that can be collected from third parties on their behalf, and funds that are available to the taxpayer but not subject to IRS collection actions.

The taxpayer may choose to pay the offer amount in a lump sum, in monthly payments over the remainder of the statutory time allowed for collection or a combination of a lump sum and monthly payments. Generally, it is to the taxpayer's advantage to pay the amount in the shortest amount of time possible. Nevertheless, the IRS cannot consider an offer in compromise if the taxpayer is involved in an open bankruptcy proceeding or if they have not filed all federal tax returns.

IRS Taxpayer Advocate Program

The IRS offers special assistance on unresolved tax matters which are causing the taxpayer to suffer hardship. If the taxpayer is suffering, or is about to suffer a significant hardship because of the way Internal Revenue laws are being carried out against them, they may ask for special help from the IRS Taxpayer Advocate Program. However, before requesting this assistance the taxpayer should first attempt to use the existing administrative or formal appeal procedures. Most problems are resolved through regular channels. However, if any of the following circumstances apply, the taxpayer may ask for assistance from the Taxpayer Advocate Program:

1. The taxpayer is suffering or about to suffer a significant hardship.

2. The taxpayer is facing an immediate threat of adverse action.

3. The taxpayer will incur significant costs if relief is not granted, including fees for professional representation.

4. The taxpayer will suffer irreparable injury or long term adverse impact if relief is not granted.

5. The taxpayer has experienced a delay of more than 30 calendar days to resolve a tax-related problem or inquiry.

6. The taxpayer has not received a response or resolution to their problem by the date promised.

7. A system(s) or procedure(s) has either failed to operate as intended or failed to resolve the taxpayer's problem or dispute within the IRS.

If one or more of the above circumstances applies, the Taxpayer Advocate may issue a Taxpayer Assistance Order to suspend, delay, stop, or speed up IRS actions to relieve the taxpayer's hardship. Taxpayer Advocates cannot change the tax law or make a technical tax decision, however, they can clear up problems that resulted from previous contacts and ensure that the taxpayer's case is given a complete and impartial review. The IRS Tax-payer Advocate Program may be reached by calling 1-877-777-4778 (1-877-PRP-IRSU).

CHAPTER 5:
DEBT COLLECTION HARASSMENT

IN GENERAL

In most instances, people do not intentionally fail to pay their valid debts. Studies have shown that the primary reasons people fall into debt are loss of employment, health reasons, or a change in family status, such as divorce. These scenarios are certain to be a source of great stress to an individual who previously was able to responsibly manage his or her finances.

Thus, the debtor is quite vulnerable to the often abusive tactics used by debt collectors. The consequences can be devastating. The emotional stress can lead to serious physical conditions, such as ulcers and heart attacks. A debt collector who continually telephones a debtor at his place of employment can jeopardize the debtor's job.

Recognizing the serious nature of this problem, federal and state laws have been enacted to protect the debtor from illegal collection tactics. The debtor is entitled to take legal action against the offending debt collector. Different statutes afford the debtor different types of relief.

The prohibited practices and available remedies under the federal Fair Debt Collection Practices Act are set forth below. In addition, state statutes may provide the debtor with additional relief. Depending on the violation, the debtor may be able to pursue remedies under both federal and state law. The reader is advised to consult the law of his or her own jurisdiction to determine the relief available under state law.

New York State's debt collection harassment statute is set forth at Appendix 9 as an example of a state statute prohibiting debt collection harassment.

ALTERNATIVES TO LITIGATION

If the debtor wishes to put an end to debt collection harassment but does not necessarily want to sue, there are a number of alternatives which may be explored. For example, the debtor can request, in writing, that there be no further contact concerning the debt. Once such a written request is received, a collection agency must comply.

The letter should be sent to the collection agency by certified mail with a return receipt requested. This will give the debtor written proof of the date the collection agency received the letter. Copies of the letter should be sent to the original creditor, and to the appropriate state and federal agencies.

A sample Notice to Collection Agency to Cease Contact is set forth at Appendix 5.

If the debtor's request is not honored, the next letter should come from an attorney, with a warning that legal action will be taken if the contact continues. Of course, prior to litigation, the debtor can also attempt to settle the debt.

GATHERING EVIDENCE

Sometimes the debt collector's behavior is so egregious, and such a blatant violation of the debt collection laws, that it should be challenged. Of course, one needs proof to pursue a lawsuit, otherwise it would be the debtor's word against the collector. Thus, it is important for the debtor to keep accurate notes of every telephone call received by the debt collector. The notes should include the times and dates of the telephone calls, the name and telephone number of the person making the contact, and the actual language used by the collector, including quotes of any particularly threatening or abusive statements.

Depending on the law of the jurisdiction, it may be legal to tape the conversations you have with debt collectors, without telling them that they are being taped. Most answering machines now have the capability of taping a telephone conversation. If there are debt collectors telephoning you who are violating the law—e.g., using profane and threatening language—a tape recording will certainly bolster your case if you decide to take legal action against them.

Of course, it is essential for the reader to check the laws of his or her jurisdiction on the legality of taping without consent, so as to avoid violating any statutes. It is generally considered unethical for an attorney to tape a telephone conversation without the knowledge of all parties.

If the law prevents taping the telephone conversation, an alternative would be to have a third party—as a potential witness—listen to the conversation on an extension or by way of three-way calling. The witness should take detailed notes concerning the conversation.

In addition, if you continue to receive collection letters dated after the return receipt date of your notice to cease contact, this may indicate a violation has taken place. Save all of the correspondence you receive from the debt collection agency for review by your attorney.

COMMON-LAW THEORIES OF RECOVERY

In addition to the remedies available under federal and state law, the debtor can seek further relief under a number of common-law legal theories. A common law tort action may give the debtor broader recovery because the debtor's relief is not confined to that provided for in the statute. For example, depending on the jurisdiction, if the debtor is able to prove malicious, willful or reckless conduct, punitive damages may be available under the common-law.

In addition, in a common-law tort action, the debtor may be able to sue parties who would not otherwise be amenable to suit under the statutes. For example, the Fair Debt Collection Practices Act only covers debt collection agencies, and not the original creditors.

The reader is advised to check the laws of his or her jurisdiction for the specific elements which need to be proven to make out a prima facie case for each of the potential common-law actions.

Two common-law theories which are most applicable to debt collection harassment include (1) intentional infliction of emotional distress; and (2) intentional interference with business relationships.

Intentional Infliction of Emotional Distress

Intentional infliction of emotional distress is a claim of tortious—i.e., wrongful—conduct on the part of the tortfeasor which intentionally or recklessly causes mental distress to the victim. The defendant's conduct must generally be outrageous or unreasonable. Exactly what constitutes outrageous or unreasonable conduct is a question to be decided by the trier of fact. Guidelines may be found in the federal and state statutes and case law. A minority of jurisdictions may require that the emotional distress manifest in some type of physical injury.

An example of an intentional infliction of emotional distress claim is an allegation that a creditor repeatedly telephoned the debtor's home and, in speaking with the debtor and family members, used profane and threatening language, which caused the debtor and his family to suffer severe mental distress and humiliation.

Intentional Interference with Business Relationships

A common tactic used by debt collectors is to put pressure on the debtor to pay by involving his or her employer. For example, a debt collector may telephone the employer directly, or knowing that the debtor is not allowed personal calls, may place the debtor's job in jeopardy by repeatedly calling the debtor at his or her place of business. If the debtor can demonstrate that loss of employment was caused by the debt collector's actions, he or she may prevail on this theory.

Miscellaneous Common-Law Theories of Recovery

Depending on the specific factual allegations, other applicable common-law theories of recovery may include defamation, invasion of privacy, malicious prosecution, assault and battery, extortion, and fraud.

In addition, a debt collector's actions may violate state criminal laws, and statutes prohibiting the unauthorized practice of law.

ASSESSING DAMAGES

Damages commonly alleged in debt collection harassment cases include actual out-of-pocket losses, and emotional injuries, which may also manifest in physical illness. Out-of-pocket expenses may include such items as attorney fees, lost wages, and medical expenses. Most debt collection statutes include some type of statutory damages above out-of-pocket expenses.

Depending on the statute, a debtor may also be entitled to recover for the pain and suffering caused by the misconduct. Placing a dollar amount on such damages is difficult. The trier-of-fact must depend on evidence in making an award. For example, if the debtor has suffered mental distress as a result of threatening and abusive collection tactics, in addition to the debtor's own testimony, there should be testimony from a medical professional as to the existence and extent of the injury.

In addition, a debt collector's conduct may be so malicious or reckless as to warrant the assessment of punitive damages. The purpose of punitive damages is to punish the offender, and to deter similar behavior and future violations by the offender and other debt collection agencies.

CAUSATION

To prevail in a debt collection harassment case, the debtor must be able to demonstrate that his or her injuries were caused by the debt collector's illegal acts. This can present problems. For example, it can be presumed that an individual who has fallen into debt is already under stress. The debtor must be able to show how the illegal collection tactics contributed to the debtor's suffering.

In addition, the debtor may have been contacted by a number of debt collectors, some or most of whom operated within the bounds of the law. The debtor must be able to connect his or her injuries to the misconduct of the offending collectors, and the degree to which each is responsible must be analyzed.

THE FAIR DEBT COLLECTION PRACTICES ACT

In General

Many of the state debt collection harassment statutes are patterned after the Fair Debt Collection Practices Act (the "FDCPA"). In addition, the debtor may find remedies in the Federal Trade Commission Act. Section 5 of the Act governs unfair or deceptive acts or practices in connection with debt collection. The Federal Trade Commission (FTC) will investigate activities that can lead to law enforcement action

A copy of the FTC Consumer Complaint Form is set forth at Appendix 10.

In 1988, the FDCPA was enacted to supplement the available statutory and common law tort remedies available to the debtor to restrain unfair debt collection procedures. The FDCPA contains detailed provisions regulating the manner in which debt collection is carried out. However, the FDCPA applies only to debt collection agencies whereas the state statutes modeled after the FDCPA generally apply to creditors as well. Attorneys are not included in the definition of debt collector under the FDCPA.

Personal, family, and household debts are covered under the FDCPA, including money owed for the purchase of an automobile, for medical care, or for charge accounts.

Obligations of Debt Collectors Under the FDCPA

The FDCPA requires debt collectors to provide information about the alleged debt, and verification of the debt, at the request of the consumer, including the name of the creditor, the amount of the debt, and an offer to provide the name of the original creditor, if different.

In addition, a statement must be sent, generally with the first communication, advising the debtor that the debt will be assumed valid if he or she fails to dispute its validity within 30 days, and that any disputed debt will be verified by the debt collector with the credit grantor.

A sample letter to a credit card issuer disputing an item reported by the credit grantor is set forth at Appendix 11.

Prohibited Practices Under the FDCPA

The FDCPA prohibits various kinds of collection practices, including, but not limited to:

1. Communicating with the debtor at an unusual or inconvenient time or place;

2. Communicating with the debtor at his or her place of employment if the employer prohibits such communications, or if the debtor requests that he or she not be contacted there;

3. Communicating with a debtor who is represented by an attorney;

4. Communicating with third parties without the authorization of the debtor;

5. Communicating with the debtor after he or she has notified the debt collector to cease communication concerning the debt. In this case, the debt collector may not contact the debtor except for the limited purpose of advising the debtor, in writing, of further action to be taken;

6. Making false, deceptive or misleading representations;

7. Using unfair or unconscionable conduct to collect the debt; and

8. Using harassing, threatening or otherwise abusive conduct to collect the debt.

If the debtor has an attorney, the debt collector must contact the attorney, rather than the debtor. If the debtor does not have an attorney, a collector may contact other people, but only to find out where the debtor lives, what their phone number is, and where they work. Collectors are usually prohibited from contacting such third parties more than once. In most cases, the collector may not tell anyone other than the debtor and their attorney that the debtor owes money.

In addition, a debt collector may not contact the debtor if, within 30 days after the debtor receives written notice of the debt, they send the collection agency a letter stating they do not owe money. However, a collector can renew collection activities if they send you proof of the debt, such as a copy of a bill for the amount owed. A debt collector may not apply a payment to any debt the debtor believes they do not owe. If the debtor owes more than one debt, any payment they make must be applied to the debt they indicate.

Remedies Under the FDCPA

If a debt collector violates any of the provisions of the FDCPA, he or she is liable to the person with whom the violation took place. This would include the debtor and any other persons who were subject to the debt collector's improper tactics. The statute of limitations on bringing an action under the FDCPA is one year.

The debtor is entitled to actual damages, including physical or emotional injury, and actual expenses. The debtor is also entitled to statutory damages of up to One Thousand ($1,000.00) Dollars as set forth in the Act, whether or not actual damages exist, and whether or not the violation was intentional or inadvertent. Debtors who prevail on their claim may also be entitled to legal fees and costs at the discretion of the court.

The text of the Fair Debt Collection Practices Act is set forth at Appendix 12 and a sample Complaint brought under the FDCPA for debt collection harassment is set forth at Appendix 13.

CHAPTER 6:
CREDIT REHABILITATION

CREDIT REPORTING AGENCIES

When a consumer applies for credit, such as a credit card, or an automobile loan, etc., he or she generally fills out an application form which sets forth information concerning the consumer's creditworthiness. In considering the application, the creditor generally requests a report from a credit reporting agency to (i) verify the information, (ii) obtain additional information concerning the consumer's ability to take on additional debt, and (iii) obtain the consumer's credit payment history, e.g. whether the consumer is a late or timely payor.

All major credit granters routinely supply credit reporting agencies information concerning the payment history of its customers. The credit reporting agency also searches public records to determine whether the consumer has any judgments or liens filed which would affect their creditworthiness. The three major national credit bureaus are:

1. Equifax, P.O. Box 740241, Atlanta, GA 30374-0241; (800) 685-1111.

2. Experian (formerly TRW), P.O. Box 2104, Allen, TX 75013; (888) EXPERIAN (397-3742).

3. Trans Union, P.O. Box 1000, Chester, PA 19022; (800) 916-8800.

When one is unable to pay his or her debts on time, late payments and other adverse action—such as judgments and liens—will appear on one's credit report. Negative information, such as delinquent accounts, judgments, liens, or charge-offs, is supposed to be deleted after seven years.

The seven year period starts to run from the date of the negative activity. For example, a delinquent account may be reported as delinquent for seven years from the date it becomes delinquent. If the delinquency subsequently becomes a charge-off, it may be reported as a charge-off for seven years from that date.

There are certain exceptions to, and extensions of, the seven-year rule, so the reader is advised to check the statute. The most common exceptions include the following:

1. Bankruptcy information may be reported for 10 years.

2. Information reported in response to an application for a job with a salary of more than $75,000 has no time limit.

3. Information reported because of an application for more than $150,000 worth of credit or life insurance has no time limit.

4. Information about a lawsuit or an unpaid judgment can be reported for seven years or until the statute of limitations runs out, whichever is longer.

Credit reporting agencies are obligated to make sure the information contained in the consumer's file is current. The rationale for this requirement is to give the consumer a chance to rehabilitate a negative credit history. Maintaining information in this manner is helpful to both creditor and consumer provided it is accurate, and maintained in a manner so as to protect the applicant's privacy rights.

For example, the consumer must authorize the creditor to obtain his or her credit report. Unauthorized release of credit information may result in an action for invasion of the consumer's right to privacy. In addition, inaccurate information, such as negligently reporting the consumer as a late payor, may result in a defamation action. Nevertheless, both of these remedies have their shortcomings when applied to consumer actions.

THE FAIR CREDIT REPORTING ACT

In response to the inadequacy of the common law remedies for unfair credit reporting activities, Congress enacted the Fair Credit Reporting Act (the "FCRA") in 1970 as Subchapter III of its Consumer Credit Protection Act. The FCRA preempts any state statutes which are inconsistent with its provisions.

Under the FCRA, creditors—defined as "users"—may only obtain a consumer's credit report for limited purposes, the most common of which are extension of credit or employment. In addition, a creditor may only request a credit report for the individual consumer involved in the transaction, and cannot obtain a spouse's credit report if the spouse is not a party to the transaction. It is a crime under the FCRA to obtain a consumer's credit report under false pretenses.

If the credit reporting agency willfully or negligently issues a report to a person who does not have a permissible purpose in obtaining the report, the agency is subject to civil liability. An individual employee who knowingly and willingly issues the report may be subject to criminal sanctions.

The FCRA also requires credit reporting agencies to maintain accurate information, and to permit consumers to correct any inaccuracies found in their reports. However, a credit reporting agency is not subject to civil liability for inaccuracies contained in consumer credit reports provided they "follow reasonable procedures to assure maximum possible accuracy of the information. . . ." Nevertheless, if the credit reporting agency does not follow "reasonable procedures," they may be subject to liability.

If the consumer disputes the accuracy of information contained in his or her file, the agency is required to reinvestigate this information within a reasonable period of time. If, upon reinvestigation, the information cannot be verified, or is proven inaccurate, it must be deleted, and corrected copies must be sent to all parties who recently requested copies of the report. However, if the agency believes upon reinvestigation that the information is accurate, the consumer is entitled to include a statement of dispute in the report.

A sample letter to a credit reporting agency disputing information contained in a credit report is set forth at Appendix 14.

A credit reporting agency or user is liable to the consumer for any actual damages suffered as a result of negligence. Actual damages generally include monetary losses and have also been held to include damages for mental anguish resulting from aggravation, embarrassment, humiliation and injury to reputation, etc. Further, if the violation is willful, punitive damages may also be available to the consumer.

OBTAINING LEGAL SERVICES

At various stages of indebtedness, one may want to retain a lawyer. A lawyer can contact creditors and try to establish a payment plan which will work within the debtor's budget. A lawyer may also be able to settle a debt—even after it has become a judgment—for an amount considerably less than the original debt. Although the individual debtor can attempt to negotiate a settlement, an attorney letter generally receives a more immediate response.

If a creditor is assured that they will be paid in a lump sum payment, they are often willing to negotiate. The last thing the creditor wants is for the debtor to declare bankruptcy. Thereafter, the chance of recovering any part of the debt is slim or nonexistent.

A lawyer should also be consulted if the debtor has been victimized by unscrupulous debt collection practices. As further discussed in Chapter 5, debtors have statutory and common-law rights to take legal action for debt collection harassment.

Finally, if served with legal papers, the debtor should consult a lawyer immediately.

CREDIT COUNSELING SERVICES

There are a number of companies which claim to offer credit counseling services. It is important to do a background check on a company before making an appointment. A legitimate credit counseling service is generally a nonprofit organization which employs counselors who are knowledgeable about credit and debt collection. Credit counseling agencies may also offer educational materials and workshops.

The credit counselor acts as an intermediary between the creditor and debtor. He or she reviews the debtor's financial picture and helps the debtor prepare a debt repayment plan to pay off his or her debts over a period of time. The counselor is usually able to get the creditor to waive finance and late payment charges so that the debtor need only repay the principal balance due. Once a budget has been established, the debtor generally pays one monthly payment to the service, which apportions the money among the creditors. The service usually requires the debtor to surrender all of his or her credit cards in order to be eligible for assistance.

There is usually no charge for the credit counseling. Some credit counseling agencies charge little or nothing for managing the plan while others charge a monthly fee that could add up to a significant charge over time. A successful repayment plan requires you to make regular, timely payments, and could take 48 months or longer to complete.

A debt repayment plan does not erase your credit history and creditors will continue to report information about accounts that are handled through a debt repayment plan. For example, creditors may report that an account is in financial counseling, that payments have been missed, or that there are write-offs or other concessions. But a demonstrated pattern of timely payments should help you get credit in the future.

HOUSING COUNSELING AGENCIES

If you fall behind on your mortgage, contact your lender immediately to avoid foreclosure. Most lenders will work with you if they believe you're acting in good faith and the situation is temporary. Some lenders may reduce or suspend mortgage payments for a short time. Lenders may also agree to change the terms of the mortgage by extending the repayment period to reduce the monthly payments.

If you cannot work out a plan with your lender, you may consider contacting a housing counseling agency. Some agencies limit their counseling services to homeowners with FHA mortgages, but many offer free help to any homeowner having trouble making mortgage payments. The homeowner should call the local office of the Department of Housing and Urban Development (HUD) or the housing authority in your state, city, or county for help in finding a housing counseling agency near you.

DEBT CONSOLIDATION ADVERTISEMENTS

The Federal Trade Commission (FTC) cautions consumers to read between the lines when faced with ads that advise the consumer to "consolidate their bills into one monthly payment without borrowing." Such advertisements often involve bankruptcy proceedings, which can seriously hurt one's credit rating and cost an already debt-burdened consumer to incur attorneys' fees. Although bankruptcy is sometimes the only alternative available, it should be used as a last resort after all other means of paying one's debts have been investigated.

CREDIT REPAIR SERVICES

There are companies which claim that they can re-establish a good credit rating for the debtor—for a fee—despite how bad one's credit may be. It is generally best to avoid any companies that claim the ability to turn a bad credit report into a good one. The companies who advertise that they can erase bad credit are generally in business to earn a profit by undertaking actions that the individual can handle on their own. For example, if one's credit report includes negative information which is outdated, or contains inaccurate information, the credit reporting agency, by law, must correct the inaccuracy. It is not necessary to pay someone to have this information deleted. This can easily be handled by the individual.

If, however, the negative credit report reflects legitimately owed debts, neither the debtor nor a credit repair service would be able to convince a credit reporting agency, or creditor, to report otherwise. Only time, a conscientious effort, and a personal debt repayment plan can improve a poor credit record.

The companies that advertise credit repair services appeal to consumers with poor credit histories. They cannot repair credit and, in fact, their tactics may be illegal and may also engage the consumer in illegal activity, such as asking the consumer to make false statements on credit applications, and fraudulently misrepresenting the consumer's social security number.

According to the Federal Trade Commission, consumer must be aware of companies that:

1. Want you to pay for credit repair services before any services are provided;

2. Do not tell you your legal rights and what you can do—yourself—for free;

3. Recommend that you not contact a credit bureau directly;

4. Suggest that you try to invent a "new" credit report by applying for an Employer Identification Number to use instead of your Social Security Number; or

5. Advise you to dispute all information in your credit report or take any action that seems illegal, such as creating a new credit identity.

If you follow illegal advice and commit fraud, you may be subject to prosecution such as mail or wire fraud if you use the mail or telephone to apply for credit and provide false information.

THE CREDIT REPAIR ORGANIZATIONS ACT

Under the Credit Repair Organizations Act, credit repair organizations must give the consumer a copy of the "Consumer Credit File Rights Under State and Federal Law" before they sign a contract with the company. In addition, they also must give the consumer a written contract that spells out all of their rights and obligations. The law contains specific protections. For example, a credit repair company cannot:

1. Make false claims about their services;

2. Charge the consumer until they have completed the promised services; or

3. Perform any services until they have your signature on a written contract and have completed a three-day waiting period. During this time, you can cancel the contract without paying any fees.

In addition, the contract must specify:

1. The payment terms for services, including their total cost;

2. A detailed description of the services to be performed;

3. How long it will take to achieve the results;

4. Any guarantees they offer; and

5. The company's name and business address.

The text of the Credit Repair Organizations Act is set forth at Appendix 15.

CHAPTER 7:
IDENTITY THEFT

IN GENERAL

Victims of identity theft are not only victimized by the criminal who misappropriated their identity, but are further victimized by the system when their credit rating is ruined through no fault of their own as they try to undo the damage caused by unauthorized procurement of credit in their name.

One may first become aware that they are the victim of identity theft when they notice that they are being billed for items they never purchased, or a credit account they never opened appears on their credit report. Perpetrators of identity theft generally misappropriate another's social security number and other personal information, without that person's knowledge or consent, to open credit accounts and incur debts. Identity theft is a crime and unfortunately it is becoming increasingly more prevalent.

Following are some of the ways identity thieves get an individual's personal information:

1. They steal wallets and purses containing your identification and credit and bank cards.

2. They steal your mail, including your bank and credit card statements, pre-approved credit offers, telephone calling cards and tax information.

3. They complete a "change of address form" to divert your mail to another location.

4. They rummage through your trash, or the trash of businesses, for personal data in a practice known as "dumpster diving."

5. They fraudulently obtain your credit report by posing as a landlord, employer or someone else who may have a legitimate need for—and a legal right to—the information.

6. They get your business or personnel records at work.

7. They find personal information in your home.

8. They use personal information you share on the Internet.

9. They buy your personal information from "inside" sources. For example, an identity thief may pay a store employee for information about you that appears on an application for goods, services or credit.

10. They call your credit card issuer and, pretending to be you, ask to change the mailing address on your credit card account. The imposter then runs up charges on your account. Because your bills are being sent to the new address, it may take some time before you realize there's a problem.

11. They open a new credit card account, using your name, date of birth and social security number. When they use the credit card and don't pay the bills, the delinquent account is reported on your credit report.

12. They establish phone or wireless service in your name.

13. They open a bank account in your name and write bad checks on that account.

14. They file for bankruptcy under your name to avoid paying debts they've incurred under your name, or to avoid eviction.

15. They counterfeit checks or debit cards, and drain your bank account.

16. They buy cars by taking out auto loans in your name.

RECOMMENDED ACTION

According to the Federal Trade Commission, if someone has stolen your identity, you should take the following three steps immediately:

1. Contact the fraud departments of each of the three major credit bureaus. Tell them to flag your file with a fraud alert including a statement that creditors should get your permission before opening any new accounts in your name. Also ask the credit bureaus for copies of your credit reports. Credit bureaus must give you a free copy of your report if it is inaccurate because of fraud. Review your reports carefully to make sure no additional fraudulent accounts have been opened in your name or unauthorized changes made to your existing accounts. In a few months, order new copies of your reports to verify your corrections and changes, and to make sure no new fraudulent activity has occurred.

2. Contact the creditors for any accounts that have been tampered with or opened fraudulently. Ask to speak with someone in the security or fraud department, and follow up in writing. Following up with a letter is one of the procedures spelled out in the Fair Credit Billing Act for resolving errors on credit billing statements, including charges that you have not made.

3. File a report with your local police or the police in the community where the identity theft took place. Keep a copy in case your creditors need proof of the crime.

If an identity thief has stolen your mail for access to new credit cards, bank and credit card statements, pre-approved credit offers and tax information or falsified change-of-address forms, he or she has committed a crime. Report it to your local postal inspector.

If you discover that an identity thief has changed the billing address on an existing credit card account, close the account. When you open a new account, ask that a password be used before any inquiries or changes can be made on the account. Avoid using easily available information like your mother's maiden name, your birth date, the last four digits of your SSN or your phone number, or a series of consecutive numbers. Avoid the same information and numbers when you create a Personal Identification Number (PIN).

If you have reason to believe that an identity thief has accessed your bank accounts, checking account or ATM card, close the accounts immediately. When you open new accounts, insist on password-only access. If your checks have been stolen or misused, stop payment. Also contact the major check verification companies to request that they notify retailers using their databases not to accept these checks, or ask your bank to notify the check verification service with which it does business. Some of the major check verification companies include:

1. National Check Fraud Service: 1-843-571-2143

2. SCAN: 1-800-262-7771

3. TeleCheck: 1-800-710-9898 or 927-0188

4. CrossCheck: 1-707-586-0551

5. Equifax Check Systems: 1-800-437-5120

6. International Check Services: 1-800-526-5380

If your ATM card has been lost, stolen or otherwise compromised, cancel the card and get another with a new PIN.

If an identity thief has established new phone or wireless service in your name and is making unauthorized calls that appear to come from-and are billed to-your cellular phone, or is using your calling card and PIN, contact your service provider immediately to cancel the account and calling card. Get new accounts and new PINs.

If it appears that someone is using your SSN when applying for a job, get in touch with the Social Security Administration (SSA) to verify the accuracy of your reported earnings and that your name is reported correctly. In addition, the SSA may issue you a new SSN at your request if, after trying to resolve the problems brought on by identity theft, you continue to experience problems. However, consider this option carefully. A new SSN may not resolve your identity theft problems, and may actually create new problems. For example, a new SSN does not necessarily ensure a new credit record because credit bureaus may combine the credit records from your old SSN with those from your new SSN. Even when the old credit information is not associated with your new SSN, the absence of any credit history under your new SSN may make it more difficult for you to get credit. And finally, there's no guarantee that a new SSN wouldn't also be misused by an identity thief. The Social Security Administration may be reached at (800) 772-1213.

If you suspect that your name or SSN is being used by an identity thief to get a driver's license, report it to your Department of Motor Vehicles. Also, if your state uses your SSN as your driver's license number, ask to substitute another number.

PREVENTING IDENTITY THEFT

Although it may be impossible to completely prevent identity theft, there are some things an individual can do to try and lessen the chances that he or she will become a victim of this crime. For example, before revealing personal identifying information, such as a social security number, one should find out how it will be used and if it will be shared with others. Inquire as to whether the requested information is mandatory or necessary. Find out what measures will be taken to keep personal information confidential.

One should also minimize the identification information and the number of cards they carry with them and keep personal information in a safe place. If your wallet and/or credit cards are lost or stolen, notify the creditors by phone immediately, and call the credit bureaus to ask that a "fraud alert" be placed in your file. In addition, check your credit report regularly—at least once a year—to make sure there are no unauthorized accounts appearing on the report.

INTERNET SERVICE PROVIDERS

If you receive an e-mail request that appears to be from your Internet Service Provider (ISP) stating that your "account information needs to be updated" or that "the credit card you signed up with is invalid or expired and the information needs to be reentered to keep your account active," do not respond without checking with your ISP first. According to information received by the Federal Trade Commission, this may be a trick to induce the individual into providing personal information that can be used to steal one's identity and procure unauthorized credit.

THE FEDERAL TRADE COMMISSION

The Federal Trade Commission (FTC) is the federal clearinghouse for complaints by victims of identity theft. Although the FTC does not have the authority to bring criminal cases, it does assist victims of identity theft by providing them with information to help them resolve the financial and other problems that can result from identity theft. The FTC also may refer victim complaints to other appropriate government agencies and private organizations for further action.

If you've been a victim of identity theft, file a complaint with the FTC by contacting the FTC's Identity Theft Hotline toll-free at 1-877-IDTHEFT (438-4338); TDD: 202-326-2502. The FTC's mailing address is: Identity Theft Clearinghouse, Federal Trade Commission, 600 Pennsylvania Avenue, NW, Washington, DC 20580. You can also contact the FTC online at: http://www.consumer.gov/idtheft.

A copy of the FTC Identity Theft Complaint Input Form is set forth at Appendix 16.

THE IDENTITY THEFT AND ASSUMPTION DETERRENCE ACT

In October 1998, Congress passed the Identity Theft and Assumption Deterrence Act of 1998 to address the problem of identity theft. Specifically, the Act amended 18 U.S.C. § 1028 to make it a federal crime when anyone knowingly transfers or uses, without lawful authority, a means of identification of another person with the intent to commit, or to aid or abet, any unlawful activity that constitutes a violation of Federal law, or that constitutes a felony under any applicable State or local law. Under the Act, a name or SSN is considered a "means of identification: as is a credit card number, cellular telephone electronic serial number or any other piece of information that may be used alone or in conjunction with other information to identify a specific individual.

In most instances, a conviction for identity theft carries a maximum penalty of 15 years imprisonment, a fine and forfeiture of any personal property used or intended to be used to commit the crime. The Act also directs the U.S. Sentencing Commission to review and amend the federal sentencing guidelines to provide appropriate penalties for those persons convicted of identity theft.

Schemes to commit identity theft or fraud also may involve violations of other statutes, such as credit card fraud; computer fraud; mail fraud; wire fraud; financial institution fraud; or Social Security fraud. Each of these federal offenses is a felony and carries substantial penalties—in some cases, as high as 30 years in prison, fines and criminal forfeiture. Violations of the Act are investigated by federal investigative agencies such as the U.S. Secret Service, the FBI, and the U.S. Postal Inspection Service and prosecuted by the Department of Justice.

In addition to the federal laws, many states have passed laws related to identity theft and others may be considering such legislation. Where specific identity theft laws do not exist, the practices may be prohibited under other laws,

A table of states with identity theft statutes is set forth at appendix 17.

IDENTITY THEFT AFFIDAVIT

The Federal Trade Commission has developed the ID Theft Affidavit as a new consumer assistance initiative designed to address identity theft. If a consumer is disputing fraudulent debts and accounts opened by an identity thief, the ID Theft Affidavit now simplifies the process. Instead of completing different forms, the consumer can use the ID Theft Affidavit to alert companies where a new account was opened in their name. The company can then investigate the fraud and decide the outcome of the consumer's claim.

A copy of the ID Theft Affidavit is set forth at Appendix 18.

Some of the Companies and Organizations that accept or endorse the ID Theft Affidavit include:

1. ACA International

2. American Bankers Association

3. Bank of America

4. Call for Action

5. Chase Manhattan Bank

6. Computer Sciences Corporation

7. Council of Better Business Bureaus

8. Direct Marketing Association

9. Equifax

10. Experian

11. Federal Reserve Board

12. First National Bank Omaha

13. GE Capital

14. Identity Theft Resource Center

15. Privacy Rights Clearinghouse

16. Providian

17. SBC Service

18. Sears

APPENDIX 1:
AGREEMENT TO ASSUME OBLIGATION

BE IT KNOWN, for good consideration, this Agreement is entered into on *[Insert Date]*, between *[Name of Creditor]* ("Creditor"), *[Name of Customer]* ("Customer"), and *[Name of Person Assuming Debt]* (the "Undersigned").

It is hereby acknowledged and agreed that:

1. Customer presently owes Creditor the sum of *[Dollar Amount ($xxx)]* Dollars (the "Debt"), which sum is fully due and payable.

2. The undersigned unconditionally and irrevocably agrees to assume and fully pay said Debt and otherwise guarantee to both Creditor and Customer the prompt payment of said debt on the terms below, and to fully indemnify and save harmless Creditor and Customer from any loss thereto.

3. Said Debt shall be promptly paid in the manner following:

[Set forth details for payment of debt].

4. This agreement shall not constitute a release or discharge of the obligations of Customer to Creditor for the payment of said Debt, provided that so long as the undersigned shall promptly pay the Debt in the manner above described, Creditor shall forebear commencing collection action against Customer.

5. In the event of default of payment, Creditor shall have full rights, jointly and severally, against both Customer and/or undersigned for any balance then owing.

6. This Agreement extends only to the above debt and to no other or greater obligation.

7. This agreement shall be binding upon and inure to the benefit of the parties, their successors, assigns and personal representatives.

BY: _____
[SIGNATURE LINE—CREDITOR]

BY: _____

[SIGNATURE LINE—CUSTOMER]

BY: _____

[SIGNATURE LINE—PARTY ASSUMING DEBT]

APPENDIX 2:
TABLE OF STATE STATUTES GOVERNING DEBT COLLECTION

STATE	STATUTE
Alabama	Alabama Code §40-12-80
Alaska	Alaska Statutes §§8.24.0.011 et. seq.
Arizona	Arizona Revised Statutes Annotated §§32-1001 et. seq.
Arkansas	Arkansas Statutes Annotated §617-21-104 et. seq.
California	California Civil Code §§1788 et. seq.
Colorado	Colorado Revised Statutes §§5-10101 et. seq; 12-14-101 et. seq.
Connecticut	Connecticut General Statutes Annotated §§36-243.a et. seq; 42-127 et. seq.
Delaware	Delaware Code Annotated, Title 30, §2301(13).
District of Columbia	D.C. Code Annotated §§22-3423 et. seq; 28-3814 et. seq.
Florida	Florida Statutes §§559.55 et. seq.
Georgia	Georgia Code Annotated §§7-3-1 et. seq.
Hawaii	Hawaii Revised Statutes §§443-B-1 et. seq.
Idaho	Idaho Code §§26-2222 et. seq.
Illinois	Illinois Annotated Statutes, Chapter 111, §§2001 et. seq.
Indiana	Indiana Code Annotated §§25-11-1-1 et. seq.
Iowa	Iowa Code Annotated §§537.7101 et. seq.
Kansas	Kansas Statutes Annotated §16a-5-107.
Kentucky	None.

STATE	STATUTE
Louisiana	Louisiana Revised Statutes Annotated §§9:3510 et. seq.
Maine	Maine Revised Statutes Annotated, Title 32 §§11, 001 et. seq; Title 9-A §§1.101 et. seq.
Maryland	Maryland Annotated Code, Article 56 §§323 et. seq; Maryland Com. Law Code Annotated, §§14-201 et. seq.
Massachusetts	Massachusetts General Laws Annotated, Chapter 93 §§24 et. seq; §49.
Michigan	Michigan Compiled Laws Annotated §19.655; §18.425.
Minnesota	None.
Missouri	None.
Montana	None.
Nebraska	Nebraska Revised Statutes §§45-601 et. seq; 45-175 et. seq.
Nevada	Nevada Revised Statutes §§649.005 et. seq.
New Hampshire	New Hampshire Revised Statutes Annotated §§358-C:1 et. seq.
New Jersey	New Jersey Statutes Annotated §§45:18-1 et. seq.
New Mexico	New Mexico Statutes Annotated §§61-18A-1 et. seq.
New York	New York General Law §§600 et. seq.
North Carolina	North Carolina General Statutes §§66-49.24 et. seq; 75-50 et. seq.
North Dakota	North Dakota Cent. Code §§13-05-01 et. seq.
Ohio	None.
Oklahoma	None.
Oregon	Oregon Revised Statutes §§646.639 et. seq; 697.010 et. seq.
Pennsylvania	18 Pennsylvania Cons. Statutes Annotated §§7311; 201-1 et. seq.
Rhode Island	None.
South Carolina	South Carolina Code Annotated §37-5-108.
South Dakota	None.
Tennessee	Tennessee Code Annotated §§62-20-101 et. seq.
Texas	Texas Revised Civ. Statutes Annotated, Arts. 5069-11.01 et. seq.

STATE	STATUTE
Utah	Utah Code Annotated §§12-1-1 et. seq.
Vermont	Vermont Statutes Annotated, Title 9 §§2451a et. seq.
Virginia	Virginia Code Annotated §§18.2 et. seq.
Washington	Washington Revised Code Annotated §§19.16.100 et. seq.
West Virginia	West Virginia Code §§47-16-1 §§18.2 et. seq; 46A-2-101 et. seq.
Wisconsin	Wisconsin Statutes Annotated §§218.04; 427.101 et. seq.
Wyoming	Wyoming Statutes §§33-11-101 et. seq.

APPENDIX 3:
CREDITOR DEMAND LETTER

Mr. John Smith
123 Main Street
White Plains, New York

RE: Charge-A-Lot Account Number 032773

Dear Mr. Smith:

We have been retained by Charge-A-Lot, Inc. to collect the amount of Three Hundred ($300.00) Dollars which is outstanding on your account. To avoid further action, please send a check or money order for the full amount immediately.

Unless you notify us within thirty days after receipt of this letter that you dispute the validity of this debt, we will assume the debt is valid. If within that time period you notify us that you dispute the debt, or any portion of it, we will obtain verification of the debt from the creditor and send it to you, and will provide you with the name and address of the original creditor if it differs from the current creditor. This letter is an attempt to collect the debt, and any information contained will be used for that purpose.

If you would like to discuss this claim further, please contact the undersigned.

Very truly yours,

Mary Jones, Collection Supervisor
The Pay Now or Else Debt Collection Agency, Inc.

APPENDIX 4:
PAYMENT AGREEMENT CONFIRMATION LETTER

Mr. John Smith
123 Main Street
White Plains, New York

RE: Charge-A-Lot Account Number 032773

Dear Mr. Smith:

This letter is being sent to you to confirm your agreement to make payments on the above-referenced account so as to avoid further action being taken against you to collect this debt.

As agreed, the outstanding balance of Three Hundred ($300.00) Dollars will be paid in equal monthly installments of Fifty ($50.00) Dollars, beginning on the first of next month, for the next six months until paid in full.

If this letter accurately states the terms of our agreement, please sign where indicated below and return the letter to me in the enclosed self-addressed stamped envelope.

Very truly yours,

Mary Jones, Collection Supervisor
The Pay Now or Else Debt Collection Agency, Inc.

ACKNOWLEDGED BY_____
                                John Smith

APPENDIX 5:
NOTICE TO COLLECTION AGENCY TO CEASE CONTACT

[Date]

BY CERTIFIED MAIL—RETURN RECEIPT REQUESTED

TO: [The Pay Now or Else Debt Collection Agency, Inc.]

RE: Charge-A-Lot Account Number 032773

Dear Sir/Madam:

This letter shall serve as a notice to your company to cease any further contact with me in connection with the above-referenced account. As I am sure you are aware, the law requires you to comply with this request.

I am presently unable to make payments on this account because [state reasons, e.g., illness, layoff, etc.]. I am trying to reorganize my financial situation, and intend to take care of this matter as soon as I am able. Although I have explained my circumstances to your employees, they have continued to employ collection tactics which are illegal. [Give details]. This has caused me a great amount of stress.

I would appreciate your cooperation so as to avoid having to assert my legal rights in a court of law. Thank you.

Very truly yours,

John Smith

cc: Charge-A-Lot, Inc.
cc: The Federal Trade Commission
cc: The Better Business Bureau

APPENDIX 6:
AGREEMENT TO COMPROMISE A DEBT

BE IT KNOWN, for good and valuable consideration, I, *[Name of Creditor]* ("Creditor"), as a creditor of *[Name of Debtor]* ("Debtor"), hereby enter into this agreement to compromise and discharge the indebtedness due from Debtor to Creditor on the following terms and conditions:

[Specify terms and conditions, e.g.: Payment must be made within 15 days of the date of this agreement.]

The Debtor and Creditor acknowledge that the present debt due and owing Creditor is in the amount of *[Dollar Amount ($xxx)]* Dollars.

The parties agree that the undersigned creditor shall accept the sum of *[Dollar Amount ($xxx)]* Dollars as full and total payment on said debt and in complete discharge, release, satisfaction and settlement of all monies presently due, provided the sum herein shall be fully and punctually paid in the following manner: *[Specify manner of payment, e.g., by certified check or money order, etc.].*

In the event the Debtor fails to fully and punctually pay the compromised amount, Creditor shall have full rights to prosecute Creditor's claim for the full amount of *[Dollar Amount ($xxx)]* Dollars, less credits for payments made.

In the event of default in payment the Debtor agrees to pay all reasonable attorneys' fees and costs of collection.

This agreement shall be binding upon and inure to the benefit of the parties, their successors, assigns and personal representatives.

DATED:

BY: _____
    [SIGNATURE LINE—DEBTOR]

DATED:

BY: _____
    [SIGNATURE LINE—CREDITOR]

APPENDIX 7:
SATISFACTION OF JUDGMENT AND
RELEASE OF LIEN

BE IT KNOWN, that *[Name of Beholder]* ("Lienholder"), of *[Address]*, con-tracted with *[Name of Contracting Party]* on *[Date of Contract]*, to furnish labor and/or materials for construction on the premises owned by *[Name of Property Owner]*, located at *[Address]*.

On *[Date of Filing]*, the lienholder filed a notice of lien against the above property in the Office of the County Clerk, County of _____, in the State of _____. Said lien was duly recorded in *[Set forth recording information]* of the Lien Records of the County.

In consideration of *[Dollar Amount ($xxx)]* Dollars, receipt of which is ac-knowledged, lienholder releases the above described property and the owner personally from all liability arising from the labor performed and/or materials furnished by lienholder under the terms of the above-mentioned contract, and authorizes and directs that the above-mentioned lien be dis-charged of record.

DATED:

BY: _____
    [SIGNATURE LINE—LIENHOLDER]

STATE OF   )

    ss.:

COUNTY OF   )

On the ___ day of _____, 20___, before me personally came *[Name of Lienholder]*, to me known to be the individual described in and who exe-cuted the foregoing instrument, and acknowledged that he/she executed the same.

_____
[NOTARY PUBLIC]

APPENDIX 8:
IRS INSTALLMENT AGREEMENT REQUEST

Form **9465**
(Rev. November 2000)
Department of the Treasury
Internal Revenue Service (99)

Installment Agreement Request

▶ If you are filing this form with your tax return, attach it to the front of the return. Otherwise, see instructions.

OMB No. 1545-1350

Caution: Do not file this form if you are currently making payments on an installment agreement. You must pay your other Federal tax liabilities in full or you will be in default on your agreement.

1 Your first name and initial — Last name — Your social security number

If a joint return, spouse's first name and initial — Last name — Spouse's social security number

Your current address (number and street). If you have a P.O. box and no home delivery, enter your box number. — Apt. number

City, town or post office, state, and ZIP code. If a foreign address, enter city, province or state, and country. Follow the country's practice for entering the postal code.

2 If this address is new since you filed your last tax return, check here . . . . ▶ ☐

3 ( ) Your home phone number — Best time for us to call   4 ( ) Your work phone number — Ext. — Best time for us to call

5 Name of your bank or other financial institution: 6 Your employer's name:

Address   Address

City, state, and ZIP code   City, state, and ZIP code

(TIP) If you are filing this form in response to a notice, do not complete lines 7 through 9. Instead, attach the bottom section of the notice to this form and go to line 10.

7 Enter the tax return for which you are making this request (for example, Form 1040) . . . . . . ▶ **7**

8 Enter the tax year for which you are making this request (for example, 2000) . . . . ▶ **8**

9 Enter the total amount you owe as shown on your tax return **9**

10 Enter the amount of any payment you are making with your tax return (or notice). See instructions **10**

11 Enter the amount you can pay each month. **Make your payments as large as possible to limit interest and penalty charges.** The charges will continue until you pay in full **11**

12 Enter the date you want to make your payment each month. **Do not** enter a date later than the 28th. . ▶ **12**

13 If you want to make your payments by direct debit, see the instructions and fill in lines 13a, 13b, and 13c.

▶ **a** Routing number ☐☐☐☐☐☐☐☐☐   ▶ **c** Type: ☐ Checking ☐ Savings

▶ **b** Account number ☐☐☐☐☐☐☐☐☐☐☐☐☐☐☐☐☐

I authorize the U.S. Treasury and its designated Financial Agent to initiate a monthly ACH debit (electronic withdrawal) entry to the financial institution account indicated for payments of my Federal taxes owed, and the financial institution to debit the entry to this account. This authorization is to remain in full force and effect until I notify the U.S. Treasury Financial Agent to terminate the authorization. To revoke payment, I must contact the U.S. Treasury Financial Agent at **1-800-829-8815** no later than 7 business days prior to the payment (settlement) date. I also authorize the financial institutions involved in the processing of the electronic payments of taxes to receive confidential information necessary to answer inquiries and resolve issues related to the payments.

Your signature — Date   Spouse's signature. If a joint return, **both** must sign — Date

General Instructions

Section references are to the Internal Revenue Code.

Purpose of Form

Use Form 9465 to request a monthly installment plan if you cannot pay the full amount you owe shown on your tax return (or on a notice we sent you). But before requesting an installment agreement, you should consider other less costly alternatives, such as a bank loan. If you have any questions about this request, call 1-800-829-1040.

Your request for an installment agreement cannot be turned down if the tax you owe is not more than $10,000 and **all three** of the following apply.

1. During the past 5 tax years, you (and your spouse if you are making a request for a joint tax return) have timely filed all income tax returns and

paid any income tax due, and have not entered into an installment agreement for payment of income tax.

2. The IRS determines that you cannot pay the tax owed in full when it is due and you give the IRS any information needed to make that determination.

3. You agree to pay the full amount you owe within 3 years and to comply with the tax laws while the agreement is in effect.

[!] *A Notice of Federal Tax Lien may be filed to protect the government's interest until you pay in full.*

Bankruptcy or Offer-in-Compromise. If you are in bankruptcy or we have accepted your offer-in-compromise, **do not** file this form. Instead, call 1-800-829-1040 to get the number of your local IRS Insolvency function for bankruptcy or Technical Support function for offer-in-compromise.

For Privacy Act and Paperwork Reduction Act Notice, see back of form.   Cat. No. 14842Y   Form **9465** (Rev. 11-2000)

IRS INSTALLMENT AGREEMENT REQUEST

What Will You Be Charged

You will be charged a $43 fee if your request is approved. **Do not include the fee with this form.** After approving your request, we will bill you for the fee with your first payment.

You will also be charged interest and may be charged a late payment penalty on any tax not paid by its due date, even if your request to pay in installments is granted. To limit interest and penalty charges, file your return on time and pay as much of the tax as possible with your return (or notice).

How Does the Installment Agreement Work

If we approve your request, we will send you a letter. It will tell you how to pay the fee and make your first installment payment. We will usually let you know within 30 days after we receive your request whether it is approved or denied. But if this request is for tax due on a return you filed after March 31, it may take us longer than 30 days to reply.

By approving your request, we agree to let you pay the tax you owe in monthly installments instead of immediately paying the amount in full. In return, you agree to make your monthly payments on time. **You also agree to meet all your future tax liabilities.** This means that you must have enough withholding or estimated tax payments so that your tax liability for future years is paid in full when you timely file your return.

After we receive each payment, we will send you a letter showing the remaining amount you owe, and the due date and amount of your next payment. But if you choose to have your payments automatically withdrawn from your bank account, you will not receive a letter. Your bank statement is your record of payment. We will also give you a statement showing the amount you owe at the beginning of the year, all payments made during the year, and the amount you owe at the end of the year.

If you **do not** make your payments on time or you have an outstanding past-due amount in a future year, you will be in default on your agreement and we may take enforcement actions to collect the entire amount you owe.

Where To File

Attach Form 9465 to the front of your return and send it to the address shown in your tax return booklet. If you have already filed your return or you are filing this form in response to a notice, file Form 9465 by itself with the **Internal Revenue Service Center** at the address below for the place where you live. No street address is needed.

IF you live in. . .	THEN use this address. . .
Florida, Georgia, South Carolina, West Virginia	Atlanta, GA 39901
Delaware, New Jersey, New York *(New York City and counties of Nassau, Rockland, Suffolk, and Westchester)*	Holtsville, NY 00501
New York *(all other counties)*, Connecticut, Maine, Massachusetts, New Hampshire, Rhode Island, Vermont	Andover, MA 05501
Illinois, Iowa, Kansas, Minnesota, Missouri, Oregon, Wisconsin	Kansas City, MO 64999
District of Columbia, Indiana, Maryland, Pennsylvania, Virginia	Philadelphia, PA 19255
Michigan, Ohio	Cincinnati, OH 45999
Colorado, Idaho, Montana, New Mexico, Oklahoma, Texas, Wyoming	Austin, TX 73301
Arizona, California *(counties of Alpine, Amador, Butte, Calaveras, Colusa, Contra Costa, Del Norte, El Dorado, Glenn, Humboldt, Lake, Lassen, Marin, Mendocino, Modoc, Napa, Nevada, Placer, Plumas, Sacramento, San Joaquin, Shasta, Sierra, Siskiyou, Solano, Sonoma, Sutter, Tehama, Trinity, Yolo, and Yuba)*, Nevada, North Dakota, South Dakota, Utah, Washington	Ogden, UT 84201
California *(all other counties)*, Alaska, Hawaii	Fresno, CA 93888
Alabama, Arkansas, Kentucky, Louisiana, Mississippi, Nebraska, North Carolina, Tennessee	Memphis, TN 37501

If you live in American Samoa or Puerto Rico *(or exclude income under section 933)*; are a nonpermanent resident of Guam or the Virgin Islands*; have an APO, FPO, or foreign address; are a dual-status alien; or file Form 2555, 2555-EZ, or 4563, use this address: *Internal Revenue Service Center, Philadelphia, PA 19255.*

*Permanent residents of Guam and the Virgin Islands cannot use Form 9465.

Specific Instructions

Line 1

If you are making this request for a joint tax return, show the names and social security numbers (SSNs) in the same order as on your tax return.

Line 10

Even if you cannot pay the full amount you owe now, you should pay as much as possible to limit penalty and interest charges. If you are filing this form with your tax return, make the payment with your return. For details on how to pay, see your tax return instructions.

If you are filing this form **by itself**, such as in response to a notice, attach a check or money order payable to the **"United States Treasury."** **Do not send cash.** Be sure to include:

- Your name, address, SSN, and daytime phone number.
- The tax year and tax return (for example, "2000 Form 1040") for which you are making this request.

Line 11

You should try to make your payments large enough so that your balance due will be paid off by the due date of your next tax return.

Line 12

You can choose the date your monthly payment is due. For example, if your rent or mortgage payment is due on the first of the month, you may want to make your installment payments on the 15th. When we approve your request, we will tell you the month and date that your first payment is due.

If we have not replied by the date you chose for your first payment, you may send the first payment to the Internal Revenue Service Center at the address shown on this page that applies to you. See the instructions for line 10 to find out what to write on your payment.

Lines 13a Through 13c

Instead of sending us a check each month, you can pay by direct debit (electronic withdrawal) from your account at a bank or other financial institution (such as mutual fund, brokerage firm, or credit union). To do so, fill in lines 13a, 13b, and 13c. Check with your financial institution to make sure that a direct debit is allowed and to get the correct routing and account numbers.

Note: *We will send you a bill for the first payment and the fee. All other payments will be electronically withdrawn.*

Line 13a. The first two digits of the routing number must be 01 through 12 or 21 through 32. Do not use a deposit slip to verify the number because it may contain internal routing numbers that are not part of the actual routing number.

Line 13b. The account number can be up to 17 characters (both numbers and letters). Include hyphens but omit spaces and special symbols. Enter the number from left to right and leave any unused boxes blank. Be sure **not** to include the check number.

Privacy Act and Paperwork Reduction Act Notice. Our legal right to ask for the information on this form is sections 6001, 6011, 6012(a), 6109, and 6159 and their regulations. We will use the information to process your request for an installment agreement. The reason we need your name and social security number is to secure proper identification. We require this information to gain access to the tax information in our files and properly respond to your request. If you do not enter the information, we may not be able to process your request.

You are not required to provide the information requested on a form that is subject to the Paperwork Reduction Act unless the form displays a valid OMB control number. Books or records relating to a form or its instructions must be retained as long as their contents may become material in the administration of any Internal Revenue law. Generally, tax returns and return information are confidential, as required by section 6103. However, we may give this information to the Department of Justice as provided by law. We may also give it to cities, states, and the District of Columbia to carry out their tax laws.

The time needed to complete and file this form will vary depending on individual circumstances. The estimated average time is: **Learning about the law or the form,** 7 min.; **Preparing the form,** 26 min.; and **Copying, assembling, and sending the form to the IRS,** 20 min.

If you have comments concerning the accuracy of this time estimate or suggestions for making this form simpler, we would be happy to hear from you. You can write to the Tax Forms Committee, Western Area Distribution Center, Rancho Cordova, CA 95743-0001. **Do not send the form to this address. Instead, see Where To File on this page.**

APPENDIX 9:
NEW YORK GENERAL BUSINESS
LAW—ARTICLE 29

SECTION 600. DEFINITIONS

As used in this article, unless the context or subject matter otherwise requires:

1. "Consumer claim" means any obligation of a natural person for the payment of money or its equivalent which is or is alleged to be in default and which arises out of a transaction wherein credit has been offered or extended to a natural person, and the money, property or service which was the subject of the transaction was primarily for personal, family or household purposes. The term includes an obligation of a natural person who is a co-maker, endorser, guarantor or surety as well as the natural person to whom such credit was originally extended.

2. "Debtor" means any natural person who owes or who is asserted to owe a consumer claim.

3. "Principal creditor" means any person, firm corporation or organization to whom a consumer claim is owed, due or asserted to be due or owed, or any assignee for value of said person, firm corporation or organization.

SECTION 601. PROHIBITED PRACTICES

No principal creditor, as defined by this article, or his agent shall:

1. Simulate in any manner a law enforcement officer, or a representative of any governmental agency of the state of New York or any of its political subdivisions; or

2. Knowingly collect, attempt to collect, or assert a right to any collection fee, attorney's fee, court cost or expense unless such charges are justly due and legally chargeable against the debtor; or

3. Disclose or threaten to disclose information affecting the debtor's reputation for credit worthiness with knowledge or reason to know that the information is false; or

4. Communicate or threaten to communicate the nature of a consumer claim to the debtor's employer prior to obtaining final judgment against the debtor. The provisions of this subdivision shall not prohibit a principal creditor from communicating with the debtor's employer to execute a wage assignment agreement if the debtor has consented to such an agreement; or

5. Disclose or threaten to disclose information concerning the existence of a debt known to be disputed by the debtor without disclosing that fact; or

6. Communicate with the debtor or any member of his family or household with such frequency or at such unusual hours or in such a manner as can reasonably be expected to abuse or harass the debtor; or

7. Threaten any action which the principal creditor in the usual course of his business does not in fact take; or

8. Claim, or attempt or threaten to enforce a right with knowledge or reason to know that the right does not exist; or

9. Use a communication which simulates in any manner legal or judicial process or which gives the appearance of being authorized, issued or approved by a government, governmental agency, or attorney at law when it is not.

SECTION 602. VIOLATIONS AND PENALTIES

1. Except as otherwise provided by law, any person who shall violate the terms of this article shall be guilty of a misdemeanor, and each such violation shall be deemed a separate offense.

2. The attorney general or the district attorney of any county may bring an action in the name of the people of the state to restrain or prevent any violation of this article or any continuance of any such violation.

SECTION 603. SEVERABILITY

If any provision of this article or the application thereof to any person or circumstances is held invalid the invalidity thereof shall not affect other provisions or applications of the article which can be given effect without the invalid provision or application, and to this end the provisions of this article are severable.

APPENDIX 10:
FTC CONSUMER COMPLAINT FORM

Complaint Input Form

 **FTC Consumer Complaint Form**

OMB #3084-0

Use this form to submit a complaint to the Federal Trade Commission (FTC) Bureau of Consumer Protection about a particular company or organization. The information you provide is up to you. However, if you do not provide your name or other information, it may be impossible for us to refer, respond to, or investigate your complaint or request. To learn how we use the information you provide, please read our Privacy Policy.

While the FTC does not resolve individual consumer problems, your complaint helps us investigate fraud, and can lead to law enforcement action. The FTC enters Internet, telemarketing, identity theft and other fraud-related complaints into Consumer Sentinel, a secure, online database available to hundreds of civil and criminal law enforcement agencies worldwide.

We use secure socket layer (SSL) encryption to protect the transmission of the information you submit. The information you provide is stored securely offline.

IMPORTANT: If you would like to submit a report about **Identity Theft**, please use our Identity Theft Complaint Form.

If you would like to forward **unsolicited commercial e-mail** (spam) to the Commission, please send it directly to UCE@FTC.GOV without using this form.

If your complaint is about an online related transaction and involves a foreign company, please use our econsumer.gov complaint form.

Page 1

Complaint Input Form

How Do We Reach You?

First Name: [_____]

Last Name: [_____]

Age Range: [_____ ▲▼] "Click" Arrow for Choices

Street Address: [_____]
[_____]

City: [_____]

State or Canadian Province: [_____ ▲▼] "Click" Arrow for Choices

Country: [_____ ▲▼] "Click" Arrow for Choices

Zip Code or Postal Code: [_____]

E-Mail Address: [_____]

Home Phone: [____] -[_____]

Work Phone: [____] -[_____] Ext.[____]

Tell Us Your Complaint...

Subject of Your Complaint: [_____ ▲▼]
"Click" Arrow for Choices

Name of Company You Are Complaining About: [_____]

Check If Company Name Is Unknown: ☐

Street Address: [_____]
[_____]

City: [_____]

State or Canadian Province: [_____ ▲▼] "Click" Arrow for Choices

Country: [_____ ▲▼] "Click" Arrow for Choices

Zip Code or Postal Code: [_____]

Company Web Site: [_____]

Company E-Mail Address: [_____] Page 2

Complaint Input Form

Phone Number: [   ] - [   ] Ext.[   ]

How Did the
Company Initially
Contact You?: [   ] [⬍] "Click" Arrow for Choices

How Much Did the
Company Ask You
to Pay?: [   ]

How Much Did You
Actually Pay the
Company?: [   ]

How Did You Pay
the Company?: [   ] [⬍] "Click" Arrow for Choices

REPRESENTATIVE
OR SALESPERSON [   ]
First Name:

Last Name: [   ]

Date Company
Contacted You: [   ] (MM/DD/YYYY)

Explain Your
Problem: (Please
limit your
complaint to 2000
characters.) [   ]

[Submit Complaint] [Clear Form]

Paperwork Reduction Statement: This form is designed to improve public access to the FTC Bureau of Consumer Protection Consumer Response Center, and is voluntary. Through this form, consumers may electronically register a complaint with the FTC. We estimate that it will take, on average, 5 minutes to complete the form. Under the Paperwork Reduction Act, as amended, an agency may not conduct or sponsor, and a person is not required to respond to, a collection of information unless it displays a currently valid OMB control number. That number is 3084-0047, which also appears in the upper right-hand corner of the first page of this form

APPENDIX 11:
CREDIT CARD ISSUER ITEM DISPUTE LETTER

[Name of Credit Card Issuer]
[Address]
[City, State, Zip Code]

Attn: Billing Inquiries

I am writing to dispute a billing error in the amount of $_____on my account. The amount is inaccurate because (describe the problem). I am requesting that the error be corrected, that any finance and other charges related to the disputed amount be credited as well, and that I receive an accurate statement.

Enclosed are copies of (use this sentence to describe any enclosed information, such as sales slips, payment records) supporting my position. Please investigate this matter and correct the billing error as soon as possible.

Sincerely,

John Doe

Enclosures: (List what you are enclosing.)

APPENDIX 12:
FAIR DEBT COLLECTION PRACTICES ACT

15 USCS § 1692. CONGRESSIONAL FINDINGS AND DECLARATION OF PURPOSE

(a) Abusive practices.

There is abundant evidence of the use of abusive, deceptive, and unfair debt collection practices by many debt collectors. Abusive debt collection practices contribute to the number of personal bankruptcies, to marital instability, to the loss of jobs, and to invasions of individual privacy.

(b) Inadequacy of laws.

Existing laws and procedures for redressing these injuries are inadequate to protect consumers.

(c) Available non-abusive collection methods.

Means other than misrepresentation or other abusive debt collection practices are available for the effective collection of debts.

(d) Interstate commerce.

Abusive debt collection practices are carried on to a substantial extent in interstate commerce and through means and instrumentalities of such commerce. Even where abusive debt collection practices are purely intrastate in character, they nevertheless directly affect interstate commerce.

(e) Purposes.

It is the purpose of this title to eliminate abusive debt collection practices by debt collectors, to insure that those debt collectors who refrain from using abusive debt collection practices are not competitively disadvantaged, and to promote consistent State action to protect consumers against debt collection abuses.

SECTION 1692a. DEFINITIONS

As used in this title:

(1) The term "Commission" means the Federal Trade Commission.

(2) The term "communication" means the conveying of information regarding a debt directly or indirectly to any person through any medium.

(3) The term "consumer" means any natural person obligated or allegedly obligated to pay any debt.

(4) The term "creditor" means any person who offers or extends credit creating a debt or to whom a debt is owed, but such term does not include any person to the extent that he receives an assignment or transfer of a debt in default solely for the purpose of facilitating collection of such debt for another.

(5) The term "debt" means any obligation or alleged obligation of a consumer to pay money arising out of a transaction in which the money, property, insurance, or services which are the subject of the transaction are primarily for personal, family, or household purposes, whether or not such obligation has been reduced to judgment.

(6) The term "debt collector" means any person who uses any instrumentality of interstate commerce or the mails in any business the principal purpose of which is the collection of any debts, or who regularly collects or attempts to collect, directly or indirectly, debts owed or due or asserted to be owed or due another. Notwithstanding the exclusion provided by clause (F) of the last sentence of this paragraph, the term includes any creditor who, in the process of collecting his own debts, uses any name other than his own which would indicate that a third person is collecting or attempting to collect such debts. For the purpose of section 808(6) [15 USCS § 1692f(6)], such term also includes any person who uses any instrumentality of interstate commerce or the mails in any business the principal purpose of which is the enforcement of security interests. The term does not include:

(A) any officer or employee of a creditor while, in the name of the creditor, collecting debts for such creditor;

(B) any person while acting as a debt collector for another person, both of whom are related by common ownership or affiliated by corporate control, if the person acting as a debt collector does so only for persons to whom it is so related or affiliated and if the principal business of such person is not the collection of debts;

(C) any officer or employee of the United States or any State to the extent that collecting or attempting to collect any debt is in the performance of his official duties;

(D) any person while serving or attempting to serve legal process on any other person in connection with the judicial enforcement of any debt;

(E) any nonprofit organization which, at the request of consumers, performs bona fide consumer credit counseling and assists consumers in the liquidation of their debts by receiving payments from such consumers and distributing such amounts to creditors; and

(F) any person collecting or attempting to collect any debt owed or due or asserted to be owed or due another to the extent such activity (i) is incidental to a bona fide fiduciary obligation or a bona fide escrow arrangement; (ii) concerns a debt which was originated by such person; (iii) concerns a debt which was not in default at the time it was obtained by such person; or (iv) concerns a debt obtained by such person as a secured party in a commercial credit transaction involving the creditor.

(G) [Redesignated]

(7) The term "location information" means a consumer's place of abode and his telephone number at such place, or his place of employment.

(8) The term "State" means any State, territory, or possession of the United States, the District of Columbia, the Commonwealth of Puerto Rico, or any political subdivision of any of the foregoing.

SECTION 1692b. ACQUISITION OF LOCATION INFORMATION.

Any debt collector communicating with any person other than the consumer for the purpose of acquiring location information about the consumer shall:

(1) identify himself, state that he is confirming or correcting location information concerning the consumer, and, only if expressly requested, identify his employer;

(2) not state that such consumer owes any debt;

(3) not communicate with any such person more than once unless requested to do so by such person or unless the debt collector reasonably believes that the earlier response of such person is erroneous or incomplete and that such person now has correct or complete location information;

(4) not communicate by postcard;

(5) not use any language or symbol on any envelope or in the contents of any communication effected by the mails or telegram that indicates that the debt collector is in the debt collection business or that the communication relates to the collection of a debt; and

(6) after the debt collector knows the consumer is represented by an attorney with regard to the subject debt and has knowledge of, or can readily ascertain, such attorney's name and address, not communicate with any person other than that attorney, unless the attorney fails to respond within a reasonable period of time to communication from the debt collector.

SECTION 1692c. COMMUNICATION IN CONNECTION WITH DEBT COLLECTION

(a) Communication with the consumer generally.

Without the prior consent of the consumer given directly to the debt collector or the express permission of a court of competent jurisdiction, a debt collector may not communicate with a consumer in connection with the collection of any debt:

(1) at any unusual time or place or a time or place known or which should be known to be inconvenient to the consumer. In the absence of knowledge of circumstances to the contrary, a debt collector shall assume that the convenient time for communicating with a consumer is after 8 o'clock antimeridian and before 9 o'clock postmeridian, local time at the consumer's location;

(2) if the debt collector knows the consumer is represented by an attorney with respect to such debt and has knowledge of, or can readily ascertain, such attorney's name and address, unless the attorney fails to respond within a reasonable period of time to a communication from the debt collector or unless the attorney consents to direct communication with the consumer; or

(3) at the consumer's place of employment if the debt collector knows or has reason to know that the consumer's employer prohibits the consumer from receiving such communication.

(b) Communication with third parties.

Except as provided 15 USCS §1692b, without the prior consent of the consumer given directly to the debt collector, or the express permission of a court of competent jurisdiction, or as reasonably necessary to effectuate a postjudgment judicial remedy, a debt collector may not communicate, in connection with the collection of any debt, with any person other than the consumer, his attorney, a consumer reporting agency if otherwise permitted by law, the creditor, the attorney of the creditor, or the attorney of the debt collector.

(c) Ceasing communication.

If a consumer notifies a debt collector in writing that the consumer refuses to pay a debt or that the consumer wishes the debt collector to cease further communication with the consumer, the debt collector shall not communicate further with the consumer with respect to such debt, except:

(1) to advise the consumer that the debt collector's further efforts are being terminated;

(2) to notify the consumer that the debt collector or creditor may invoke specified remedies which are ordinarily invoked by such debt collector or creditor; or

(3) where applicable, to notify the consumer that the debt collector or creditor intends to invoke a specified remedy. If such notice from the consumer is made by mail, notification shall be complete upon receipt.

(d) "Consumer" defined.

For the purpose of this section, the term "consumer" includes the consumer's spouse, parent (if the consumer is a minor), guardian, executor, or administrator.

SECTION 1692d. HARASSMENT OR ABUSE

A debt collector may not engage in any conduct the natural consequence of which is to harass, oppress, or abuse any person in connection with the collection of a debt. Without limiting the general application of the foregoing, the following conduct is a violation of this section:

(1) The use or threat of use of violence or other criminal means to harm the physical person, reputation, or property of any person.

(2) The use of obscene or profane language or language the natural consequence of which is to abuse the hearer or reader.

(3) The publication of a list of consumers who allegedly refuse to pay debts, except to a consumer reporting agency or to persons meeting the requirements of section 1681a(f) or 1681b(3)] of this title.

(4) The advertisement for sale of any debt to coerce payment of the debt.

(5) Causing a telephone to ring or engaging any person in telephone conversation repeatedly or continuously with intent to annoy, abuse or harass any person at the called number.

SECTION 1692e. FALSE OR MISLEADING REPRESENTATIONS

A debt collector may not use any false, deceptive, or misleading representation or means in connection with the collection of any debt. Without limiting the general application of the foregoing, the following conduct is a violation of this section:

(1) The false representation or implication that the debt collector is vouched for, bonded by, or affiliated with the United States or any State, including the use of any badge, uniform, or facsimile thereof.

(2) The false representation of:

(A) the character, amount, or legal status of any debt; or

(B) any services rendered or compensation which may be lawfully received by any debt collector for the collection of a debt.

(3) The false representation or implication that any individual is an attorney or that any communication is from an attorney.

(4) The representation or implication that nonpayment of any debt will result in the arrest or imprisonment of any person or the seizure, garnishment, attachment, or sale of any property or wages of any person unless such action is lawful and the debt collector or creditor intends to take such action.

(5) The threat to take any action that cannot legally be taken or that is not intended to be taken.

(6) The false representation or implication that a sale, referral, or other transfer of any interest in a debt shall cause the consumer to:

(A) lose any claim or defense to payment of the debt; or

(B) become subject to any practice prohibited by this title.

(7) The false representation or implication that the consumer committed any crime or other conduct in order to disgrace the consumer.

(8) Communicating or threatening to communicate to any person credit information which is known or which should be known to be false, including the failure to communicate that a disputed debt is disputed.

(9) The use or distribution of any written communication which simulates or is falsely represented to be a document authorized, issued, or approved by any court, official, or agency of the United States or any

State, or which creates a false impression as to its source, authorization, or approval.

(10) The use of any false representation or deceptive means to collect or attempt to collect any debt or to obtain information concerning a consumer.

(11) Except as otherwise provided for communications to acquire location information under section 1692b], the failure to disclose clearly in all communications made to collect a debt or to obtain information about a consumer, that the debt collector is attempting to collect a debt and that any information obtained will be used for that purpose.

(12) The false representation or implication that accounts have been turned over to innocent purchasers for value.

(13) The false representation or implication that documents are legal process.

(14) The use of any business, company, or organization name other than the true name of the debt collector's business, company, or organization.

(15) The false representation or implication that documents are not legal process forms or do not require action by the consumer.

(16) The false representation or implication that a debt collector operates or is employed by a consumer reporting agency as defined by section 1681a(f)] of this title.

SECTION 1692f. UNFAIR PRACTICES

A debt collector may not use unfair or unconscionable means to collect or attempt to collect any debt. Without limiting the general application of the foregoing, the following conduct is a violation of this section:

(1) The collection of any amount (including any interest, fee, charge, or expense incidental to the principal obligation) unless such amount is expressly authorized by the agreement creating the debt or permitted by law.

(2) The acceptance by a debt collector from any person of a check or other payment instrument postdated by more than five days unless such person is notified in writing of the debt collector's intent to deposit such check or instrument not more than ten nor less than three business days prior to such deposit.

(3) The solicitation by a debt collector of any postdated check or other postdated payment instrument for the purpose of threatening or instituting criminal prosecution.

(4) Depositing or threatening to deposit any postdated check or other postdated payment instrument prior to the date on such check or instrument.

(5) Causing charges to be made to any person for communications by concealment of the true purpose of the communication. Such charges include, but are not limited to, collect telephone calls and telegram fees.

(6) Taking or threatening to take any nonjudicial action to effect dispossession or disablement of property if:

(A) there is no present right to possession of the property claimed as collateral through an enforceable security interest;

(B) there is no present intention to take possession of the property; or

(C) the property is exempt by law from such dispossession or disablement.

(7) Communicating with a consumer regarding a debt by postcard.

(8) Using any language or symbol, other than the debt collector's address, on any envelope when communicating with a consumer by use of the mails or by telegram, except that a debt collector may use his business name if such name does not indicate that he is in the debt collection business.

SECTION 1692g. VALIDATION OF DEBTS

(a) Notice of debt; contents.

Within five days after the initial communication with a consumer in connection with the collection of any debt, a debt collector shall, unless the following information is contained in the initial communication or the consumer has paid the debt, send the consumer a written notice containing:

(1) the amount of the debt;

(2) the name of the creditor to whom the debt is owed;

(3) a statement that unless the consumer, within thirty days after receipt of the notice, disputes the validity of the debt, or any portion thereof, the debt will be assumed to be valid by the debt collector;

(4) a statement that if the consumer notifies the debt collector in writing within the thirty-day period that the debt, or any portion thereof, is disputed, the debt collector will obtain verification of the debt or a copy of a judgment against the consumer and a copy of such verification or judgment will be mailed to the consumer by the debt collector; and

(5) a statement that, upon the consumer's written request within the thirty-day period, the debt collector will provide the consumer with the name and address of the original creditor, if different from the current creditor.

(b) Disputed debts.

If the consumer notifies the debt collector in writing within the thirty-day period described in subsection (a) that the debt, or any portion thereof, is disputed, or that the consumer requests the name and address of the original creditor, the debt collector shall cease collection of the debt, or any disputed portion thereof, until the debt collector obtains verification of the debt or a copy of a judgment, or the name and address of the original creditor, and a copy of such verification or judgment, or name and address of the original creditor, is mailed to the consumer by the debt collector.

(c) Admission of liability.

The failure of a consumer to dispute the validity of a debt under this section may not be construed by any court as an admission of liability by the consumer.

SECTION 1692h. MULTIPLE DEBTS

If any consumer owes multiple debts and makes any single payment to any debt collector with respect to such debts, such debt collector may not apply such payment to any debt which is disputed by the consumer and, where applicable, shall apply such payment in accordance with the consumer's directions.

SECTION 1692i. LEGAL ACTIONS BY DEBT COLLECTORS

(a) Venue.

Any debt collector who brings any legal action on a debt against any consumer shall:

(1) in the case of an action to enforce an interest in real property securing the consumer's obligation, bring such action only in a judicial district or similar legal entity in which such real property is located; or

(2) in the case of an action not described in paragraph (1), bring such action only in the judicial district or similar legal entity:

(A) in which such consumer signed the contract sued upon; or

(B) in which such consumer resides at the commencement of the action.

(b) Authorization of actions.

Nothing in this title shall be construed to authorize the bringing of legal actions by debt collectors.

SECTION 1692j. FURNISHING CERTAIN DECEPTIVE FORMS

(a) It is unlawful to design, compile, and furnish any form knowing that such form would be used to create the false belief in a consumer that a person other than the creditor of such consumer is participating in the collection of or in an attempt to collect a debt such consumer allegedly owes such creditor, when in fact such person is not so participating.

(b) Any person who violates this section shall be liable to the same extent and in the same manner as a debt collector is liable under section 1692k of this title for failure to comply with a provision of this subchapter.

1692k. CIVIL LIABILITY

(a) Amount of damages.

Except as otherwise provided by this section, any debt collector who fails to comply with any provision of this title with respect to any person is liable to such person in an amount equal to the sum of:

(1) any actual damage sustained by such person as a result of such failure;

(2)(A) in the case of any action by an individual, such additional damages as the court may allow, but not exceeding $1,000; or

(2)(B) in the case of a class action, (i) such amount for each named plaintiff as could be recovered under subparagraph (A), and (ii) such amount as the court may allow for all other class members, without regard to a minimum individual recovery, not to exceed the lesser of $500,000 or 1 per centum of the net worth of the debt collector; and

(3) in the case of any successful action to enforce the foregoing liability, the costs of the action, together with a reasonable attorney's fee as determined by the court. On a finding by the court that an action under this section was brought in bad faith and for the purpose

of harassment, the court may award to defendant attorney's fees reasonable in relation to the work expended and costs.

(b) Factors considered by court.

In determining the amount of liability in any action under subsection (a), the court shall consider, among other relevant factors:

(1) in any individual action under subsection (a)(2)(A), the frequency and persistence of noncompliance by the debt collector, the nature of such noncompliance, and the extent to which such noncompliance was intentional; or

(2) in any class action under subsection (a)(2)(B), the frequency and persistence of noncompliance by the debt collector, the nature of such noncompliance, the resources of the debt collector, the number of persons adversely affected, and the extent to which the debt collector's noncompliance was intentional.

(c) Intent.

A debt collector may not be held liable in any action brought under this title if the debt collector shows by a preponderance of evidence that the violation was not intentional and resulted from a bona fide error the maintenance of procedures reasonably adapted to avoid any such error.

(d) Jurisdiction.

An action to enforce any liability created by this title may be brought in any appropriate United States district court without regard to the amount in controversy, or in any other court of competent jurisdiction, within one year from the date on which the violation occurs.

(e) Advisory opinions of Commission.

No provision of this section imposing any liability shall apply to any act done or omitted in good faith in conformity with any advisory opinion of the Commission, notwithstanding that after such act or omission has occurred, such opinion is amended, rescinded, or determined by judicial or other authority to be invalid for any reason.

SECTION 1692l. ADMINISTRATIVE ENFORCEMENT

(a) Federal Trade Commission.

Compliance with this title shall be enforced by the Commission, except to the extent that enforcement of the requirements imposed under this title is specifically committed to another agency under subsection (b). For purpose of the exercise by the Commission of its functions and powers under the Federal Trade Commission Act, a violation of this title shall be deemed an unfair or deceptive act or practice in violation of that Act. All of the functions and powers of the Commission under the Federal Trade Commission Act are available to the Commission to enforce compliance by any person with this title, irrespective of whether that person is engaged in commerce or meets any other jurisdictional tests in the Federal Trade Commission Act, including the power to enforce the provisions of this title in the same manner as if the violation had been a violation of a Federal Trade Commission trade regulation rule.

(b) Applicable provisions of law.

Compliance with any requirements imposed under this title shall be enforced under:

(1) section 8 of the Federal Deposit Insurance Act, in the case of:

(A) national banks, and Federal branches and Federal agencies of foreign banks, by the Office of the Comptroller of the Currency;

(B) member banks of the Federal Reserve System (other than national banks), branches and agencies of foreign banks (other than Federal branches, Federal agencies, and insured State branches of foreign banks), commercial lending companies owned or controlled by foreign banks, and organizations operating under section 25 or 25(a) [25A] of the Federal Reserve Act, by the Board of Governors of the Federal Reserve System; and

(C) banks insured by the Federal Deposit Insurance Corporation (other than members of the Federal Reserve System) and insured State branches of foreign banks, by the Board of Directors of the Federal Deposit Insurance Corporation;

(2) section 8 of the Federal Deposit Insurance Act, by the Director of the Office of Thrift Supervision, in the case of a savings association the deposits of which are insured by the Federal Deposit Insurance Corporation;

(3) the Federal Credit Union Act, by the Administrator of the National Credit Union Administration [National Credit Union Administration Board] with respect to any Federal credit union;

(4) the Acts to regulate commerce, by the Secretary of Transportation, with respect to all carriers subject to the jurisdiction of the Surface Transportation Board;

(5) the Federal Aviation Act of 1958, by the Secretary of Transportation with respect to any air carrier or any foreign air carrier subject to that Act; and

(6) the Packers and Stockyards Act (except as provided in section 406 of that Act, by the Secretary of Agriculture with respect to any activities subject to that Act.

(c) Agency powers.

For the purpose of the exercise by any agency referred to in subsection (b) of its powers under any Act referred to in that subsection, a violation of any requirement imposed under this title shall be deemed to be a violation of a requirement imposed under that Act. In addition to its powers under any provision of law specifically referred to in subsection (b), each of the agencies referred to in that subsection may exercise, for the purpose of enforcing compliance with any requirement imposed under this title any other authority conferred on it by law, except as provided in subsection (d).

(d) Rules and regulations.

Neither the Commission nor any other agency referred to in subsection (b) may promulgate trade regulation rules or other regulations with respect to the collection of debts by debt collectors as defined in this title.

SECTION 1692m. REPORTS TO CONGRESS BY THE COMMISSION

(a) Not later than one year after the effective date of this subchapter and at one-year intervals thereafter, the Commission shall make reports to the Congress concerning the administration of its functions under this subchapter, including such recommendations as the Commission deems necessary or appropriate. In addition, each report of the Commission shall include its assessment of the extent to which compliance with this subchapter is being achieved and a summary of the enforcement actions taken by the commission under section 1692l of this title.

(b) In the exercise of its functions under this subchapter, the Commission may obtain upon request the views of any other Federal agency which exercises enforcement functions under section 1692l of this title.

SECTION 1692n. RELATION TO STATE LAWS

This subchapter does not annul, alter, or affect, or exempt any person subject to the provisions of this subchapter from complying with the laws of any State with respect to debt collection practices, except to the extent that those laws are inconsistent with any provision of this subchapter, and then only to the extent of the inconsistency. For purposes of this section, a State law is not inconsistent with this subchapter if the protection such law affords any consumer is greater than the protection provided by this subchapter.

SECTION 1692o. EXEMPTION FOR STATE REGULATION

The Commission shall by regulation exempt from the requirements of this subchapter any class of debt collection practices within any State if the Commission determines that under the law of that State that class of debt collection practices is subject to requirements substantially similar to those imposed by this subchapter, and that there is adequate provision for enforcement.

APPENDIX 13:
COMPLAINT FOR DEBT COLLECTION HARASSMENT

[CAPTION]

COMPLAINT

I. INTRODUCTION

This is an action brought by an individual consumer for statutory damages under the Fair Debt Collection Practices Act, 15 U.S.C. Section 1692 et. seq. (hereinafter referred to as the "FDCPA"), resulting from Defendants' violations of the statute by engaging in abusive, deceptive and unfair debt collection practices.

II. JURISDICTION

The jurisdiction of this court to determine this action arises under 15 U.S.C. Section 1692k(d) and 28 U.S.C. Section 1337.

III. PARTIES

The plaintiff, John Smith, is a natural person residing at 123 Main Street, City of White Plains, County of Westchester, State of New York.

The defendant, The Pay Now or Else Debt Collection Agency, Inc. is a corporation with its principal place of business located at 1 Park Avenue, New York, New York. The defendant is engaged in the business of collecting debts on behalf of third parties.

IV. STATEMENT OF FACTS

On or about January 1, 2001, defendant telephoned plaintiff at his place of employment, demanding payment of a debt allegedly due a creditor, Charge-A-Lot, Inc., under Account Number 032773.

The plaintiff advised the defendant that he could not receive telephone calls at his place of employment. Nevertheless, the defendant telephoned the plaintiff three additional times on that same day.

Plaintiff thereafter sent a letter to defendant advising them that he did not want to be contacted concerning collection of this debt, either by telephone or in writing. This letter was sent by certified mail with a return receipt requested.

A copy of plaintiff's letter dated January 3, 2001 is attached as Exhibit A. A copy of the return receipt card signed by a representative of defendant on January 5, 2001 is attached as Exhibit B.

On February 1, 2001, defendant telephoned plaintiff at his home and spoke with his minor child. Defendant used threatening and abusive language to the child, to wit: the defendant stated that the child's father would be sent to jail if he did not pay his bills.

On February 3, 2001, defendant again telephoned plaintiff's place of employment. Plaintiff was not present at the time. Plaintiff's co-worker, Mary Jones, received the telephone call. Defendant conduct was abusive and threatening, as set forth in the affidavit of Mary Jones, attached as Exhibit C.

Defendant's violations of the statute include, but are not limited to the following:

[Specify statutory violations]

As a result of the defendant's violations of the FDCPA, plaintiff has suffered actual damages, including mental distress and medical expenses, and is entitled to an award of statutory damages, legal fees and costs.

WHEREFORE, plaintiff respectfully requests that judgment be entered against defendant as follows:

1. Actual damages;

2. Statutory damages in the amount of One Thousand ($1,000) Dollars per violation as set forth in 15 U.S.C. Section 1692k;

3. Legal fees and costs as set forth in 15 U.S.C. Section 1692k;

4. Any additional relief as to this Court appears just and reasonable.

Plaintiff requests a jury trial.

[Date]

By: _____
    [Attorney Name/Address/Telephone]

[Verification by plaintiff]

APPENDIX 14:
CREDIT REPORTING AGENCY
INFORMATION DISPUTE LETTER

[Name of Credit Reporting Agency]
[Address]
[City, State, Zip Code]

Attn: Complaint Department

Dear Sir or Madam:

I am writing to dispute the following information contained in my credit file with your Company. The items I dispute are also encircled on the attached copy of the credit report I received from your office, as follows:

Item #1: (Identify item(s) disputed by name of source, such as creditors or tax court, and identify type of item, such as credit account, judgment, etc.) This item is (inaccurate or incomplete) because (describe what is inaccurate or incomplete and why). I am requesting that the item be deleted (or request another specific change) to correct the information. Enclosed are copies of (use this sentence if applicable and describe any enclosed documentation, such as payment records, court documents) supporting my position.

Item #2: Same as above for any additional disputed information.

Please reinvestigate this (these) matter(s) and (delete or correct) the disputed item(s) as soon as possible.

Sincerely,

John Doe

Enclosures: (List what you are enclosing)

APPENDIX 15:
THE CREDIT REPAIR ORGANIZATIONS ACT

CHAPTER 2—SEC. 2451. REGULATION OF CREDIT REPAIR ORGANIZATIONS [TITLE IV OF THE CONSUMER CREDIT PROTECTION ACT (PUBLIC LAW 90-321, 82 STAT. 164)]

401. SHORT TITLE.

This title may be cited as the 'Credit Repair Organizations Act'.

402. FINDINGS AND PURPOSES.

(a) *Findings.*—The Congress makes the following findings:

(1) Consumers have a vital interest in establishing and maintaining their credit worthiness and credit standing in order to obtain and use credit. As a result, consumers who have experienced credit problems may seek assistance from credit repair organizations which offer to improve the credit standing of such consumers.

(2) Certain advertising and business practices of some companies engaged in the business of credit repair services have worked a financial hardship upon consumers, particularly those of limited economic means and who are inexperienced in credit matters.

(b) *Purposes.*—The purposes of this title are—

(1) to ensure that prospective buyers of the services of credit repair organizations are provided with the information necessary to make an informed decision regarding the purchase of such services; and

(2) to protect the public from unfair or deceptive advertising and business practices by credit repair organizations.

403. DEFINITIONS.

For purposes of this title, the following definitions apply:

(1) *Consumer.*—The term 'consumer' means an individual.

(2) *Consumer credit transaction.*—The term 'consumer credit transaction' means any transaction in which credit is offered or extended to an individual for personal, family, or household purposes.

(3) *Credit repair organization.*—The term 'credit repair organization'—

(A) means any person who uses any instrumentality of interstate commerce or the mails to sell, provide, or perform (or represent that such person can or will sell, provide, or perform) any service, in return for the payment of money or other valuable consideration, for the express or implied purpose of—

(i) improving any consumer's credit record, credit history, or credit rating; or

(ii) providing advice or assistance to any consumer with regard to any activity or service described in clause (i); and

(B) does not include—

(i) any nonprofit organization which is exempt from taxation under section 501(c)(3) of the Internal Revenue Code of 1986;

(ii) any creditor (as defined in section 103 of the Truth in Lending Act),(5) with respect to any consumer, to the extent the creditor is assisting the consumer to restructure any debt owed by the consumer to the creditor; or

(iii) any depository institution (as that term is defined in section 3 of the Federal Deposit Insurance Act) or any Federal or State credit union (as those terms are defined in section 101 of the Federal Credit Union Act), or any affiliate or subsidiary of such a depository institution or credit union.

(4) *Credit.*—The term 'credit' has the meaning given to such term in section 103(e) of this Act.

404. PROHIBITED PRACTICES.

(a) *In General.*—No person may—

(1) make any statement, or counsel or advise any consumer to make any statement, which is untrue or misleading (or which, upon the exercise of reasonable care, should be known by the credit repair organization, officer, employee, agent, or other person to be untrue or misleading) with respect to any consumer's credit worthiness, credit standing, or credit capacity to—

(A) any consumer reporting agency (as defined in section 603(f) of this Act); or

(B) any person—

(i) who has extended credit to the consumer; or

(ii) to whom the consumer has applied or is applying for an extension of credit;

(2) make any statement, or counsel or advise any consumer to make any statement, the intended effect of which is to alter the consumer's identification to prevent the display of the consumer's credit record, history, or rating for the purpose of concealing adverse information that is accurate and not obsolete to—

(A) any consumer reporting agency;

(B) any person—

(i) who has extended credit to the consumer; or

(ii) to whom the consumer has applied or is applying for an extension of credit;

(3) make or use any untrue or misleading representation of the services of the credit repair organization; or

(4) engage, directly or indirectly, in any act, practice, or course of business that constitutes or results in the commission of, or an attempt to commit, a fraud or deception on any person in connection with the offer or sale of the services of the credit repair organization.

(b).*Payment in Advance*.—No credit repair organization may charge or receive any money or other valuable consideration for the performance of any service which the credit repair organization has agreed to perform for any consumer before such service is fully performed.

405. DISCLOSURES.

(a) *Disclosure Required*.—Any credit repair organization shall provide any consumer with the following written statement before any contract or agreement between the consumer and the credit repair organization is executed:

'Consumer Credit File Rights Under State and Federal Law

You have a right to dispute inaccurate information in your credit report by contacting the credit bureau directly. However, neither you nor any "credit repair" company or credit repair organization has the right to have accurate, current, and verifiable information removed from your credit report. The credit bureau must remove accurate, negative information from your report only if it is over 7 years old. Bankruptcy information can be reported for 10 years.

You have a right to obtain a copy of your credit report from a credit bureau. You may be charged a reasonable fee. There is no fee, however, if you have been turned down for credit, employment, insurance, or a rental dwelling because of information in your credit report within the preceding 60 days. The credit bureau must provide someone to help you interpret the information in your credit file. You are entitled to receive a free copy of your credit report if you are unemployed and intend to apply for employment in the next 60 days, if you are a recipient of public welfare assistance, or if you have reason to believe that there is inaccurate information in your credit report due to fraud.

You have a right to sue a credit repair organization that violates the Credit Repair Organization Act. This law prohibits deceptive practices by credit repair organizations.

You have the right to cancel your contract with any credit repair organization for any reason within 3 business days from the date you signed it.

Credit bureaus are required to follow reasonable procedures to ensure that the information they report is accurate. However, mistakes may occur.

You may, on your own, notify a credit bureau in writing that you dispute the accuracy of information in your credit file. The credit bureau must then reinvestigate and modify or remove inaccurate or incomplete information. The credit bureau may not charge any fee for this service. Any pertinent information and copies of all documents you have concerning an error should be given to the credit bureau.

If the credit bureau's reinvestigation does not resolve the dispute to your satisfaction, you may send a brief statement to the credit bureau, to be kept in your file, explaining why you think the record is inaccurate. The credit bureau must include a summary of your statement about disputed information with any report it issues about you.

The Federal Trade Commission regulates credit bureaus and credit repair organizations. For more information contact:

> The Public Reference Branch
> Federal Trade Commission
> Washington, D.C. 20580'.

(b) *Separate Statement Requirement.*—The written statement required under this section shall be provided as a document which is separate from any written contract or other agreement between the credit repair organization and the consumer or any other written material provided to the consumer.

(c) *Retention of Compliance Records.*—

(1) *In general.*—The credit repair organization shall maintain a copy of the statement signed by the consumer acknowledging receipt of the statement.

(2) *Maintenance for 2 years.*—The copy of any consumer's statement shall be maintained in the organization's files for 2 years after the date on which the statement is signed by the consumer.

406. CREDIT REPAIR ORGANIZATIONS CONTRACTS.

(a) *Written Contracts Required.*—No services may be provided by any credit repair organization for any consumer—

(1) unless a written and dated contract (for the purchase of such services) which meets the requirements of subsection (b) has been signed by the consumer; or

(2) before the end of the 3-business-day period beginning on the date the contract is signed.

(b) *Terms and Conditions of Contract.*—No contract referred to in subsection (a) meets the requirements of this subsection unless such contract includes (in writing)—

(1) the terms and conditions of payment, including the total amount of all payments to be made by the consumer to the credit repair organization or to any other person;

(2) a full and detailed description of the services to be performed by the credit repair organization for the consumer, including—

(A) all guarantees of performance; and

(B) an estimate of—

(i) the date by which the performance of the services (to be performed by the credit repair organization or any other person) will be complete; or

(ii) the length of the period necessary to perform such services;

(3) the credit repair organization's name and principal business address; and

(4) a conspicuous statement in bold face type, in immediate proximity to the space reserved for the consumer's signature on the contract, which reads as follows: 'You may cancel this contract without penalty or obligation at any time before midnight of the 3rd business day after the date on which you signed the contract. See the attached notice of cancellation form for an explanation of this right.'.

407. RIGHT TO CANCEL CONTRACT.

(a) *In General.*—Any consumer may cancel any contract with any credit repair organization without penalty or obligation by notifying the credit repair organization of the consumer's intention to do so at any time before midnight of the 3rd business day which begins after the date on which the contract or agreement between the consumer and the credit repair organization is executed or would, but for this subsection, become enforceable against the parties.

(b) *Cancellation Form and Other Information.*—Each contract shall be accompanied by a form, in duplicate, which has the heading 'Notice of Cancellation' and contains in bold face type the following statement:

> 'You may cancel this contract, without any penalty or obligation, at any time before midnight of the 3rd day which begins after the date the contract is signed by you.

> To cancel this contract, mail or deliver a signed, dated copy of this cancellation notice, or any other written notice to (name of credit repair organization) at (address of credit repair organization) before midnight on (date).

> I hereby cancel this transaction,

> (date)

> (purchaser's signature).'.

(c) *Consumer Copy of Contract Required.*—Any consumer who enters into any contract with any credit repair organization shall be given, by the organization—

(1) a copy of the completed contract and the disclosure statement required under section 405; and

(2) a copy of any other document the credit repair organization requires the consumer to sign, at the time the contract or the other document is signed.

408. NONCOMPLIANCE WITH THIS TITLE.

(a) *Consumer Waivers Invalid.*—Any waiver by any consumer of any protection provided by or any right of the consumer under this title—

(1) shall be treated as void; and

(2) may not be enforced by any Federal or State court or any other person.

(b) *Attempt To Obtain Waiver.*—Any attempt by any person to obtain a waiver from any consumer of any protection provided by or any right of the consumer under this title shall be treated as a violation of this title.

(c) *Contracts Not in Compliance.*—Any contract for services which does not comply with the applicable provisions of this title—

(1) shall be treated as void; and

(2) may not be enforced by any Federal or State court or any other person.

409. CIVIL LIABILITY.

(a) *Liability Established.*—Any person who fails to comply with any provision of this title with respect to any other person shall be liable to such person in an amount equal to the sum of the amounts determined under each of the following paragraphs:

(1) *Actual damages.*—The greater of—

(A) the amount of any actual damage sustained by such person as a result of such failure; or

(B) any amount paid by the person to the credit repair organization.

(2) *Punitive damages.*—

(A) *Individual actions.*—In the case of any action by an individual, such additional amount as the court may allow.

(B) *Class actions.*—In the case of a class action, the sum of—

(i) the aggregate of the amount which the court may allow for each named plaintiff; and

(ii) the aggregate of the amount which the court may allow for each other class member, without regard to any minimum individual recovery.

(3) *Attorneys' fees.*—In the case of any successful action to enforce any liability under paragraph (1) or (2), the costs of the action, together with reasonable attorneys' fees.

(b) *Factors to Be Considered in Awarding Punitive Damages.*—In determining the amount of any liability of any credit repair organization under subsection (a)(2), the court shall consider, among other relevant factors—

(1) the frequency and persistence of noncompliance by the credit repair organization;

(2) the nature of the noncompliance;

(3) the extent to which such noncompliance was intentional; and

(4) in the case of any class action, the number of consumers adversely affected.

410. ADMINISTRATIVE ENFORCEMENT.

(a) *In General.*—Compliance with the requirements imposed under this title with respect to credit repair organizations shall be enforced under the Federal Trade Commission Act by the Federal Trade Commission.

(b) *Violations of This Title Treated as Violations of Federal Trade Commission Act.*—

(1) *In general.*—For the purpose of the exercise by the Federal Trade Commission of the Commission's functions and powers under the Federal Trade Commission Act, any violation of any requirement or prohibition imposed under this title with respect to credit repair organizations shall constitute an unfair or deceptive act or practice in commerce in violation of section 5(a) of the Federal Trade Commission Act.

(2) *Enforcement authority under other law.*—All functions and powers of the Federal Trade Commission under the Federal Trade Commission Act shall be available to the Commission to enforce compliance with this title by any person subject to enforcement by the Federal Trade Commission pursuant to this subsection, including the power to enforce the provisions of this title in the same manner as if the violation had been a violation of any Federal Trade Commission trade regulation rule, without regard to whether the credit repair organization—

(A) is engaged in commerce; or

(B) meets any other jurisdictional tests in the Federal Trade Commission Act.

(c) *State Action for Violations.*—

(1) *Authority of states.*—In addition to such other remedies as are provided under State law, whenever the chief law enforcement officer of a State, or an official or agency designated by a State, has reason to believe that any person has violated or is violating this title, the State—

(A) may bring an action to enjoin such violation;

(B) may bring an action on behalf of its residents to recover damages for which the person is liable to such residents under section 409 as a result of the violation; and

(C) in the case of any successful action under subparagraph (A) or (B), shall be awarded the costs of the action and reasonable attorney fees as determined by the court.

(2) *Rights of commission.*—

(A) *Notice to commission.*—The State shall serve prior written notice of any civil action under paragraph (1) upon the Federal Trade Commission and provide the Commission with a copy of its complaint, except in any case where such prior notice is not feasible, in which case the State shall serve such notice immediately upon instituting such action.

(B) *Intervention.*—The Commission shall have the right—

(i) to intervene in any action referred to in subparagraph (A);

(ii) upon so intervening, to be heard on all matters arising in the action; and

(iii) to file petitions for appeal.

(3) *Investigatory powers.*—For purposes of bringing any action under this subsection, nothing in this subsection shall prevent the chief law enforcement officer, or an official or agency designated by a State, from exercising the powers conferred on the chief law enforcement officer or such official by the laws of such State to conduct investigations or to administer oaths or affirmations or to compel the attendance of witnesses or the production of documentary and other evidence.

(4) *Limitation.*—Whenever the Federal Trade Commission has instituted a civil action for violation of this title, no State may, during the pendency of such action, bring an action under this section against any defendant named in the complaint of the Commission for any violation of this title that is alleged in that complaint.

411. STATUTE OF LIMITATIONS.

Any action to enforce any liability under this title may be brought before the later of—

(1) the end of the 5-year period beginning on the date of the occurrence of the violation involved; or

(2) in any case in which any credit repair organization has materially and willfully misrepresented any information which—

(A) the credit repair organization is required, by any provision of this title, to disclose to any consumer; and

(B) is material to the establishment of the credit repair organization's liability to the consumer under this title, the end of the 5-year period beginning on the date of the discovery by the consumer of the misrepresentation.

412. RELATION TO STATE LAW.

This title shall not annul, alter, affect, or exempt any person subject to the provisions of this title from complying with any law of any State except to the extent that such law is inconsistent with any provision of this title, and then only to the extent of the inconsistency.

413. EFFECTIVE DATE.

This title shall apply after the end of the 6-month period beginning on the date of the enactment of the Credit Repair Organizations Act,(18) except with respect to contracts entered into by a credit repair organization before the end of such period.

APPENDIX 16:
IDENTITY THEFT COMPLAINT INPUT FORM

Complaint Input Form

If you believe you have been the victim of identity theft, you may use the form below to send a complaint to the Federal Trade Commission (FTC). The information you provide is up to you. However, if you don't provide your name or other information, it may be impossible for us to refer, respond to, or investigate your complaint or request. To learn how we use the information you provide, please read our **Privacy Policy**.

The FTC serves as the federal clearinghouse for complaints by victims of identity theft. While the FTC does not resolve individual consumer problems, your complaint helps us investigate fraud, and can lead to law enforcement action. The FTC enters Internet, telemarketing, identity theft and other fraud-related complaints into Consumer Sentinel, a secure, online database available to hundreds of civil and criminal law enforcement agencies worldwide.

We use secure socket layer (SSL) encryption to protect the transmission of the information you submit. The information you provide is stored securely offline.

If you want to file a complaint with the FTC about a problem other than identity theft, please use the Federal Trade Commission online **complaint form**.

How Do We Reach You?

First Name:

Last Name:

Street Address:

Apt. or Suite No.:

City:

State/Province:

Zip:

Country:

Home Phone: Work Phone: Ext.

Social Security Number: Date Of Birth: (MM/DD/YYYY)

Email Address: [   ] (i.e., anyone@myisp.com)

Tell Us About Your Problem

1. Types of Identity Theft You Have Experienced.

ID Theft occurs when someone uses your name or other identifying information for their personal gain. Please check the types of ID theft you were a victim of. (Check as many as apply)

☐ Credit Cards   ☐ Securities or Other Investments

☐ Checking or Savings Accounts   ☐ Internet or E-Mail

☐ Loans   ☐ Government Documents or Benefits

☐ Phone or Utilities   ☐ Other

2. Describe Your Complaint Here.

Please give us information about the identity theft, including, but not limited to, how the theft occurred, who may be responsible for the theft, and what actions you have taken since the theft. Please include a list of companies where fraudulent accounts were established or your current accounts were affected. Please limit your complaint to 2000 characters.

3. Details of the Identity Theft.

When did you notice that you might be a victim of identity theft? [   ] (MM/DD/YYYY)

When did the identity theft first occur? (i.e., when was the first account opened?): [   ] (MM/DD/YYYY)

How many accounts (credit cards, loans, bank accounts, cellular phone accounts, etc.) were opened or accessed? [   ]

How much money, if any, have you had to pay? [   ]

How much money, if any, did the identity thief obtain from companies in your name? [   ]

What other problems, if any, have you experienced as a result of the identity theft? (Click on the down arrow. To select more than one, hold down the CTRL key while clicking your selection)

No Nonmonetary Damage
Civil Suit Filed or Judgement Entered Against You
Criminal Investigation, Arrest or Conviction
Denied Credit or Other Financial Services
Denied Employment or Loss of Job

4. The Identity Thief.

Please provide any information you may have about the identity thief, including his or her name, and any addresses or phone numbers the identity thief may have used.

First Name:

Last Name:

Street Address:

Apt. or Suite No.:

City:

State/Province:

Zip:

Country:

Phone Number:

E-mail Address: ....(i.e., anyone@myisp.com)

Your relationship to the identity thief:

5. Contacts.

Please indicate which of the following steps, if any, you have already taken to deal with the identity theft. For which of the following credit bureaus, have you: (check all that apply)

		Equifax		Experian		Trans Union		Other		None
Called to report the fraud?	☐	Equifax	☐	Experian	☐	Trans Union	☐	Other	☐	None
Put a "fraud alert" on your report?	☐	Equifax	☐	Experian	☐	Trans Union	☐	Other	☐	None
Ordered your credit report?	☐	Equifax	☐	Experian	☐	Trans Union	☐	Other	☐	None
Problem with Credit Bureau?	☐	Equifax	☐	Experian	☐	Trans Union	☐	Other		

Have you Contacted the police?

○ Yes

○ No

If yes, please provide police department name:

Department State:

Report Number?

○ Yes

○ No

If yes, please provide report number:

6. Problems with Companies.

Do you have any problems with the companies, credit bureaus, or organizations you are dealing with concerning your identity theft problems? If so, identify each company, credit bureau, or organization, provide its location and/or telephone number, if you have it, and tell us briefly what the problem is. **NOTE: If you checked the problem box for any of the three credit bureaus in the section above, please include those credit bureaus here.**

Company 1

Company Name:

City:

State/Province:

Zip:

Country:

Phone Number: Ext.

Have you notified this company?

○ Yes

○ No

Have you sent written notifications to this company?

○ Yes

○ No

Company 2

Company Name:

City:

State/Province:

Zip: [____]-[____]

Country: [_____]

Phone Number: [____]-[____] Ext. [____]

Have you notified this company?
- ○ Yes
- ○ No

Have you sent written notifications to this company?
- ○ Yes
- ○ No

Company 3

Company Name: [_____]

City: [_____]

State/Province: [_____]

Zip: [____]-[____]

Country: [_____]

Phone Number: [____]-[____] Ext. [____]

Have you notified this company?
- ○ Yes
- ○ No

Have you sent written notifications to this company?
- ○ Yes
- ○ No

[Reset]

Paperwork Reduction Act Statement: Paperwork Reduction Act Statement: This form is designed to improve public access to the FTC's Bureau of Consumer Protection's Consumer Response Center, and is voluntary. Through this form, consumers may electronically register a complaint with the FTC. We estimate that it will take, on average, 5 minutes to complete the form. Under the Paperwork Reduction Act, as amended, an agency may not conduct or sponsor, and a person is not required to respond to, a collection of information unless it displays a currently valid OMB control number. That number is 3084-0047, which also appears in the upper right-hand corner of the first page of this form.

APPENDIX 17:
STATES WITH IDENTITY THEFT STATUTES

STATE	STATUTE
Alabama	2001 Al. Pub. Act 312; 2001 A1. SB 144
Alaska	Alaska Stat § 11.46.180
Arizona	Ariz. Rev. Stat. § 13-2008
Arkansas	Ark. Code Ann. § 5-37-227
California	Cal. Penal Code §§ 530.5-530.7
Colorado	Colo. Rev Stat. § 18-5-102
Connecticut	1999 Gen. Stat. § 53(a)-129(a)
Delaware	Del. Code Ann. tit. II, § 854
Florida	Fla. Stat. Ann. § 817.568
Georgia	Ga. Code Ann. §§ 16-9-121, 16-9-127
Hawaii	Haw. Rev. Stat. § 708-810z
Idaho	Idaho Code § 18-3126
Illinois	720 Ill. Comp. Stat. 5/16 G
Indiana	Ind. Code Ann. § 35-43-5-4 (2000)
Iowa	Iowa Code § 715A.8
Kansas	Kan. Stat. Ann. § 21-4018
Kentucky	Ky. Rev. Stat. Ann. § 514.160
Louisiana	La. Rev. Stat. Ann. § 14:67.16
Maine	Me. Rev. Stat. Ann. tit. 17-A, § 354-2A
Maryland	Md. Code Ann. art. 27 § 231
Massachusetts	Mass. Gen. Laws ch. 266, § 37E

STATE	STATUTE
Michigan*	Mich. Comp. Laws § 750.285
Minnesota	Minn. Stat. Ann. § 609.527
Mississippi	Miss. Code Ann. § 97-19-85
Missouri	Mo. Rev. Stat. § 570.223
Montana	H.B. 331, 2001 Leg. (not yet codified)
Nevada	Nev. Rev. State. § 205.463-465
New Hampshire	N.H. Rev. Stat. Ann. § 638:26
New Jersey	N.J. Stat. Ann. § 2C:21-17
New Mexico	H.B. 317, 2001 Leg., 45th Sess.
North Carolina	N.C. Gen. Stat. § 14-113.20
North Dakota	N.D. Cent. Codes § 12.1-23
Ohio	Ohio Rev. Code Ann. § 2913.49
Oklahoma	Okla. Stat. tit. 21, § 1533.1
Oregon	Or. Rev. Stat. § 165.800
Pennsylvania	18 Pa. Cons. State § 4120
Rhode Island	R.I. Gen. Laws § 11-49.1-1
South Carolina	S.C. Code Ann. § 16-13-500, 501
South Dakota	S.D. Codified Laws § 22-30A-3.1.
Tennessee	Tenn. Code Ann. § 39-14-150
Texas	Tex. Penal Code § 32.51
Utah	Utah Code Ann. § 76-6-1101-1104
Virginia	Va. Code Ann. § 18.2-186.3
Washington	Wash. Rev. Code § 9.35.020
West Virginia	W. Va. Code § 61-3-54
Wisconsin	Wis. Stat. § 943.201
Wyoming	Wyo. Stat. Ann. § 6-3-901

Note: Where specific identity theft laws do not exist for a particular state, the practices may be prohibited under other state laws.

APPENDIX 18:
IDENTITY THEFT AFFIDAVIT

ID Theft Affidavit

Victim Information

(1) My full legal name is _____
    (First)   (Middle)   (Last)   (Jr., Sr., III)

(2) (If different from above) When the events described in this affidavit took place, I was known as

_____
(First)   (Middle)   (Last)   (Jr., Sr., III)

(3) My date of birth is _____
    (day/month/year)

(4) My social security number is_____

(5) My driver's license or identification card state and number are_____

(6) My current address is _____

City _____ State _____ Zip Code _____

(7) I have lived at this address since _____
    (month/year)

(8) (If different from above) When the events described in this affidavit took place, my address

was_____

City _____ State _____ Zip Code _____

(9) I lived at the address in #8 from _____ until _____
    (month/year)   (month/year)

(10) My daytime telephone number is (___)_____

My evening telephone number is (___)_____

Name _____ Phone number _____ Page 2

Check all that apply for items 11 - 17:

(11) ❑   I did not authorize anyone to use my name or personal information to seek the money, credit, loans, goods or services described in this report.

(12) ❑   I did not receive any benefit, money, goods or services as a result of the events described in this report.

(13) ❑   My identification documents (for example, credit cards; birth certificate; driver's license; social security card; etc.) were ❑ stolen   ❑ lost   on or about _____.
                                                                                  (day/month/year)

(14) ❑   To the best of my knowledge and belief, the following person(s) used my information (for example, my name, address, date of birth, existing account numbers, social security number, mother's maiden name, etc.) or identification documents to get money, credit, loans, goods or services without my knowledge or authorization:

_____	_____
Name (if known)	Name (if known)
_____	_____
Address (if known)	Address (if known)
_____	_____
Phone number(s) (if known)	Phone number(s) (if known)
_____	_____
additional information (if known)	additional information (if known)
_____	_____

(15) ❑   I do NOT know who used my information or identification documents to get money, credit, loans, goods or services without my knowledge or authorization.

(16) ❑   Additional comments: (For example, description of the fraud, which documents or information were used or how the identity thief gained access to your information.)

_____

_____

_____

_____

_____

(Attach additional pages as necessary.)

Name _____ Phone number _____ Page 3

(17)(check one) I ❑ am ❑ am not   willing to assist in the prosecution of the person(s) who committed this fraud.

(18)(check one) I ❑ am ❑ am not   authorizing the release of this information to law enforcement for the purpose of assisting them in the investigation and prosecution of the person(s) who committed this fraud.

(19)(check all that apply) I ❑ have ❑ have not   reported the events described in this affidavit to the police or other law enforcement agency. The police ❑ did ❑ did not write a report. *In the event you have contacted the police or other law enforcement agency, please complete the following:*

(Agency #1) _____ (Officer/Agency personnel taking report)

(Date of report) _____ (Report Number, if any)

(Phone number) _____ (e-mail address, if any)

(Agency #2) _____ (Officer/Agency personnel taking report)

(Date of report) _____ (Report Number, if any)

(Phone number) _____ (e-mail address, if any)

Please indicate the supporting documentation you are able to provide to the companies you plan to notify. Attach copies (NOT originals) to the affidavit before sending it to the companies.

(20) ❑ A copy of a valid government-issued photo-identification card (for example, your driver's license, state-issued ID card or your passport). If you are under 16 and don't have a photo-ID, you may submit a copy of your birth certificate or a copy of your official school records showing your enrollment and place of residence.

(21) ❑ Proof of residency during the time the disputed bill occurred, the loan was made or the other event took place (for example, a rental/lease agreement in your name, a copy of a utility bill or a copy of an insurance bill).

Name _____ *Phone number* _____ *Page 4*

(22) ❑ A copy of the report you filed with the police or sheriff's department. If you are unable to obtain a report or report number from the police, please indicate that in Item 19. Some companies only need the report number, not a copy of the report. You may want to check with each company.

Signature

I declare under penalty of perjury that the information I have provided in this affidavit is true and correct to the best of my knowledge.

_____   _____
(signature)   (date signed)

Knowingly submitting false information on this form could subject you to criminal prosecution for perjury.

_____
(Notary)

[Check with each company. Creditors sometimes require notarization. If they do not, please have one witness (non-relative) sign below that you completed and signed this affidavit.]

Witness:

_____   _____
(signature)   (printed name)

_____   _____
(date)   (telephone number)

Name _____ *Phone number* _____ *Page 5*

Fraudulent Account Statement

Completing this Statement

- Make as many copies of this page as you need. **Complete a separate page for each company you're notifying and only send it to that company.** Include a copy of your signed affidavit.
- List only the account(s) you're disputing with the company receiving this form. **See the example below.**
- If a collection agency sent you a statement, letter or notice about the fraudulent account, attach a copy of that document (**NOT** the original).

I declare (check all that apply):

❏ As a result of the event(s) described in the ID Theft Affidavit, the following account(s) was/were opened at your company in my name without my knowledge, permission or authorization using my personal information or identifying documents:

Creditor Name/Address *(the company that opened the account or provided the goods or services)*	Account Number	Type of unauthorized credit/goods/services provided by creditor *(if known)*	Date issued or opened *(if known)*	Amount/Value provided *(the amount charged or the cost of the goods/services)*
Example Example National Bank 22 Main Street Columbus, Ohio 22722	01234567-89	auto loan	01/05/2000	$25,500.00

❏ During the time of the accounts described above, I had the following account open with your company:

Billing name _____

Billing address _____

Account number _____

Instructions for
Completing the ID Theft Affidavit

To make certain that you do not become responsible for the debts incurred by the identity thief, you must provide proof that you didn't create the debt to each of the companies where accounts were opened or used in your name.

A working group composed of credit grantors, consumer advocates and the Federal Trade Commission (FTC) developed this ID Theft Affidavit to help you report information to many companies using just one standard form. Use of this affidavit is optional. While many companies accept this affidavit, others require that you submit more or different forms. Before you send the affidavit, contact each company to find out if they accept it.

You can use this affidavit where a **new account** was opened in your name. The information will enable the companies to investigate the fraud and decide the outcome of your claim. (If someone made unauthorized charges to an **existing account**, call the company to find out what to do.)

This affidavit has two parts:

* **ID Theft Affidavit** is where you report general information about yourself and the theft.

* **Fraudulent Account Statement** is where you describe the fraudulent account(s) opened in your name. Use a separate Fraudulent Account Statement for each company you need to write to.

When you send the affidavit to the companies, attach copies (**NOT** originals) of any supporting documents (e.g., drivers license, police report) you have.

Before submitting your affidavit, review the disputed account(s) with family members or friends who may have information about the account(s) or access to them.

Complete this affidavit as soon as possible. Many creditors ask that you send it within two weeks of receiving it. Delaying could slow the investigation.

Be as accurate and complete as possible. You *may* choose not to provide some of the information requested. However, incorrect or incomplete information will slow the process of investigating your claim and absolving the debt. Please print clearly.

When you have finished completing the affidavit, mail a copy to each creditor, bank or company that provided the thief with the unauthorized credit, goods or services you describe. Attach to each affidavit a copy of the Fraudulent Account Statement with information only on accounts opened at the institution receiving the packet, as well as any other supporting documentation you are able to provide.

Send the appropriate documents to each company by certified mail, return receipt requested, so you can prove that it was received. The companies will review your claim and send you a written response telling you the outcome of their investigation. **Keep a copy of everything you submit for your records.**

If you cannot complete the affidavit, a legal guardian or someone with power of attorney may complete it for you. Except as noted, the information you provide will be used only by the company to process your affidavit, investigate the events you report and help stop further fraud. If this affidavit is requested in a lawsuit, the company might have to provide it to the requesting party.

Completing this affidavit does not guarantee that the identity thief will be prosecuted or that the debt will be cleared.

If you haven't already done so, report the fraud to the following organizations:

1. Each of the three **national consumer reporting agencies**. Ask each agency to place a "fraud alert" on your credit report, and send you a copy of your credit file. When you have completed your affidavit packet, you may want to send them a copy to help them investigate the disputed accounts.

■ **Equifax Credit Information Services, Inc.**
(800) 525-6285 (Hearing impaired call 1-800-255-0056 and ask the operator to call the Auto Disclosure Line at 1-800-685-1111 to obtain a copy of your report.)
P.O. Box 740241, Atlanta, GA 30374-0241
www.equifax.com

■ **Experian Information Solutions, Inc.**
(888) 397-3742/ TDD (800) 972-0322
P.O. Box 9530, Allen, TX 75013
www.experian.com

■ **TransUnion**
(800) 680-7289/ TDD (877) 553-7803
Fraud Victim Assistance Division
P.O. Box 6790, Fullerton, CA 92634-6790
www.tuc.com

2. The **fraud department at each creditor, bank, or utility/service** that provided the identity thief with unauthorized credit, goods or services. This would be a good time to find out if the company accepts this affidavit, and whether they require notarization or a copy of the police report.

3. Your local **police department**. Ask the officer to take a report and give you the report number or a copy of the report. When you have completed the affidavit packet, you may want to give your police department a copy to help them add to their report and verify the crime.

4. The FTC, which maintains the Identity Theft Data Clearinghouse – the federal government's centralized identity theft complaint database – and provides information to identity theft victims. You can call toll-free **1-877-ID-THEFT (1-877-438-4338)**, visit **www.consumer.gov/idtheft**, or send mail to:

Identity Theft Data Clearinghouse
Federal Trade Commission
600 Pennsylvania Avenue, NW
Washington, DC 20580

The FTC collects complaints from identity theft victims and shares their information with law enforcement nationwide. This information also may be shared with other government agencies, consumer reporting agencies, and companies where the fraud was perpetrated to help resolve identity theft related problems.

GLOSSARY

Abuse of Process—The improper and malicious use of the criminal or civil process.

Acceptance—Acceptance refers to one's consent to the terms of an offer, which consent creates a contract.

Accord and Satisfaction -Accord and satisfaction refers to the payment of money, or other thing of value, which is usually less than the amount owed or demanded, in exchange for extinguishment of the debt.

Accrue—To occur or come into existence.

Action at Law—A judicial proceeding whereby one party prosecutes another for a wrong done.

Actionable—Giving rise to a cause of action.

Actual Damages—Actual damages are those damages directly referable to the breach or tortious act, and which can be readily proven to have been sustained, and for which the injured party should be compensated as a matter of right.

Adhesion Contract—An adhesion contract is a standardized contract form offered to consumers of goods and services on a "take it or leave it" basis without affording the consumer a realistic opportunity to bargain, and under such conditions that infer coercion.

Affirmative Defense—In a pleading, a matter constituting a defense.

American Arbitration Association (AAA)—National organization of arbitrators from whose panel arbitrators are selected for labor and civil disputes.

Annual Percentage Rate (APR)—The annual percentage rate is the actual cost of borrowing money, expressed in the form of an annual rate to make it easy for one to compare the cost of borrowing money among several lenders.

Answer—In a civil proceeding, the principal pleading on the part of the defendant in response to the plaintiff's complaint.

Anticipatory Breach of Contract—A breach committed before the arrival of the actual time of required performance.

Appearance—To come into court, personally or through an attorney, after being summoned.

Arbitration—The reference of a dispute to an impartial person chosen by the parties to the dispute who agree in advance to abide by the arbitrator's award issued after a hearing at which both parties have an opportunity to be heard.

Arbitration Clause—A clause inserted in a contract providing for compulsory arbitration in case of a dispute as to the rights or liabilities under such contract.

Arbitrator—A private, disinterested person, chosen by the parties to a disputed question, for the purpose of hearing their contention, and awarding judgment to the prevailing party.

Arrears—Payments which are due but not yet paid.

Asset—The entirety of a person's property, either real or personal.

Assignee—An assignee is a person to whom an assignment is made, also known as a grantee.

Assignment—An assignment is the transfer of an interest in a right or property from one party to another.

Bad Faith—A willful failure to comply with one's statutory or contractual obligations.

Bankrupt—The state or condition of one who is unable to pay his debts as they are, or become, due.

Bankruptcy—The legal process governed by federal law designed to assist the debtor in a new financial start while insuring fairness among creditors.

Bankruptcy Code—Refers to the Bankruptcy Act of 1978, the federal law which governs bankruptcy actions.

Bankruptcy Court—The forum in which most bankruptcy proceedings are conducted.

Bankruptcy Trustee—The person, appointed by the bankruptcy judge or selected by the creditors, who takes legal title to the property of the debtor and holds it "in trust" for equitable distribution among the creditors.

Boilerplate—Refers to standard language found almost universally in certain documents.

Breach of Contract—The failure, without any legal excuse, to perform any promise which forms the whole or the part of a contract.

Burden of Proof—The duty of a party to substantiate an allegation or issue to convince the trier of fact as to the truth of their claim.

Capacity—Capacity is the legal qualification concerning the ability of one to understand the nature and effects of one's acts.

Cause of Action—The factual basis for bringing a lawsuit.

Caveat Emptor—Latin for "let the buyer beware."

Civil Action—An action maintained to protect a private, civil right as opposed to a criminal action.

Civil Court—The court designed to resolve disputes arising under the common law and civil statutes.

Civil Law—Law which applies to non-criminal actions.

Clean Hands Doctrine—The concept that claimants who seek equitable relief must not themselves have indulged in any impropriety in relation to the transaction upon which relief is sought.

Collateral—Property which is pledged as additional security for a debt, such as a loan.

Confession of Judgment—An admission of a debt by the debtor which may be entered as a judgment without the necessity of a formal legal proceeding.

Consequential Damages -Consequential damages are those damages which are caused by an injury, but which are not a necessary result of the injury, and must be specially pleaded and proven in order to be awarded.

Consideration—Something of value exchanged between parties to a contract, which is a requirement of a valid contract.

Contract—A contract is an agreement between two or more persons which creates an obligation to do or not to do a particular thing.

Court—The branch of government responsible for the resolution of disputes arising under the laws of the government.

Credit—Credit is that which is extended to the buyer or borrower on the seller or lender's belief that that which is given will be repaid.

Credit Report—A credit report refers to the document from a credit reporting agency setting forth a credit rating and pertinent financial data concerning a person or a company, which is used in evaluating the applicant's financial stability.

Damages—In general, damages refers to monetary compensation which the law awards to one who has been injured by the actions of another, such as in the case of tortious conduct or breach of contractual obligations.

Defamation—The publication of an injurious statement about the reputation of another

Default—Default is a failure to discharge a duty or do that which ought to be done.

Defendant—In a civil proceeding, the party responding to the complaint.

Defense—Opposition to the truth or validity of the plaintiff's claims.

Demand for Arbitration—A unilateral filing of a claim in arbitration based on the filer's contractual or statutory right to do so.

Disclaimer—Words or conduct which tend to negate or limit warranty in the sale of goods, which in certain instances must be conspicuous and refer to the specific warranty to be excluded.

Down Payment—A partial payment of the purchase price.

Duress—Refers to the action of one person which compels another to do something he or she would not otherwise do.

Finance Charge—Any charge for an extension of credit, such as interest.

Fixed Income—Income which is unchangeable.

Foreclosure—The procedure by which mortgaged property is sold on default of the mortgagor in satisfaction of mortgage debt.

Fraud—A false representation of a matter of fact, whether by words or by conduct, by false or misleading allegations, or by concealment of that which should have been disclosed, which deceives and is intended to deceive another, and thereby causes injury to that person.

Fraudulent Conveyance—The transfer of property for the purpose of delaying or defrauding creditors.

Garnish—To attach the wages or property of an individual.

Garnishee—A person who receives notice to hold the assets of another, which are in his or her possession, until such time as a court orders the disposition of the property.

General Damages—General damages are those damages directly referable to the breach or tortious act and which can be readily proven to have been sustained, and for which the injured party should be compensated as a matter of right.

Grace Period—In contract law, a period specified in a contract which is beyond the due date but during which time payment will be accepted without penalty.

Guarantor—One who makes a guaranty.

Guaranty—An agreement to perform in the place of another if that person reneges on a promise contained in an underlying agreement.

Homestead—The house, outbuilding, and land owned and used as a dwelling by the head of the family.

Impound—To place property in the custody of an official.

In Rem—Refers to actions that are against property, and concerned with the disposition of that property, rather than against the person.

Indemnification Clause—An indemnification clause in a contract refers to the agreement by one party to secure the other party against loss or damage which may occur in the future in connection with performance of the contract.

Indemnify—To hold another harmless for loss or damage which has already occurred, or which may occur in the future.

Injunction—A judicial remedy either requiring a party to perform an act, or restricting a party from continuing a particular act.

Injury—Any damage done to another's person, rights, reputation or property.

Installment Contract—An installment contract is one in which the obligation, such as the payment of money, is divided into a series of successive performances over a period of time.

Interest—An amount of money paid by a borrower to a lender for the use of the lender's money.

Interest Rate—The percentage of a sum of money charged for its use.

Judge—The individual who presides over a court, and whose function it is to determine controversies.

Judgment—A judgment is a final determination by a court of law concerning the rights of the parties to a lawsuit.

Judgment Creditor—A creditor who has obtained a judgment against a debtor, which judgment may be enforced to obtain payment of the amount due.

Judgment Debtor—An individual who owes a sum of money, and against whom a judgment has been awarded for that debt.

Judgment Proof—Refers to the status of an individual who does not have the financial resources or assets necessary to satisfy a judgment.

Legal Capacity—Referring to the legal capacity to sue, it is the requirement that a person bringing the lawsuit have a sound mind, be of lawful age, and be under no restraint or legal disability.

Levy—To seize property in order to satisfy a judgment.

Liability—Liability refers to one's obligation to do or refrain from doing something, such as the payment of a debt.

Libel—The false and malicious publication, in printed form, for the purpose of defaming another.

Lien—A claim against the property of another as security for a debt. witness to the crime may attempt an identification.

Liquidated Damages—An amount stipulated in a contract as a reasonable estimate of damages to be paid in the event the contract is breached.

Loan Principal—The loan principal is the amount of the debt not including interest or any other additions.

Maker—As used in commercial law, the individual who executes a note.

Material Breach—A material breach refers to a substantial breach of contract which excuses further performance by the innocent party and gives rise to an action for breach of contract by the injured party.

Maturity Date—The date upon which a creditor is designated to receive payment of a debt, such as payment of the principal value of a bond to a bondholder by the issuing company or governmental entity.

Mechanic's Lien—A claim created by law for the purpose of securing a priority of payment of the price of work performed and materials furnished.

Mediation—The act of a third person in intermediating between two contending parties with a view to persuading them to adjust or settle their dispute but without the authority to make a binding decision.

Minor—A person who has not yet reached the age of legal competence, which is designated as 18 in most states.

Mortgage—A written instrument, duly executed and delivered, that creates a lien upon real estate as security for the payment of a specific debt.

Mutual Agreement—Mutual agreement refers to the meeting of the minds of the parties to a contract concerning the subject matter of the contract.

Negotiable Instrument—A signed writing which contains an unconditional promise to pay a sum of money, either on demand or at a specified time, payable to the order of the bearer.

Net Income—Gross income less deductions and exemptions proscribed by law.

Net Worth—The difference between one's assets and liabilities.

Nominal Damages—A trivial sum of money which is awarded as recognition that a legal injury was sustained, although slight.

Note—A writing which promises payment of a debt.

Novation—A novation refers to the substitution of a new party and the discharge of an original party to a contract, with the assent of all parties.

Obligee—An obligee is one who is entitled to receive a sum of money or performance from the obligor.

Obligor—An obligor is one who promises to perform or pay a sum of money under a contract.

Offeree—An offeree is the person to whom an offer is made.

Offeror—An offeror is the person who makes an offer.

Oral Agreement—An oral agreement is one which is not in writing or not signed by the parties.

Parties—The disputants.

Pecuniary—A term relating to monetary matters.

Performance—Performance refers to the completion of one's contractual obligation.

Referee's Deed—A deed given by a referee or other public officer pursuant to a court order for the sale of property.

Reformation—An equitable remedy which calls for the rewriting of a contract involving a mutual mistake or fraud.

Release—A document signed by one party, releasing claims he or she may have against another party, usually as part of a settlement agreement.

Repudiation—In contract law, refers to the declaration of one of the parties to the contract that he or she will not perform under the contract.

Rescission—The cancellation of a contract which returns the parties to the positions they were in before the contract was made.

Restitution—The act of making an aggrieved party whole by compensating him or her for any loss or damage sustained.

Sale—An agreement to transfer property from the seller to the buyer for a stated sum of money.

Sale and Leaseback—An agreement whereby the seller transfers property to the buyer who immediately leases the property back to the seller.

Satisfaction—The discharge and release of an obligation.

Service of Process—The delivery of legal court documents, such as a complaint, to the defendant.

Settlement—An agreement by the parties to a dispute on a resolution of the claims, usually requiring some mutual action, such as payment of money in consideration of a release of claims.

Statute of Limitations—Any law which fixes the time within which parties must take judicial action to enforce rights or thereafter be barred from enforcing them.

Stay—A judicial order suspending some action until further court order lifting the stay.

Stipulation—An admission or agreement made by parties to a lawsuit concerning the pending matter.

Subpoena—A court issued document compelling the appearance of a witness before the court.

Subpoena Duces Tecum—A court issued document requiring a witness to produce certain document in his or her possession or control.

Summons—A mandate requiring the appearance of the defendant in an action under penalty of having judgment.

Tangible Property—Property which is capable of being possessed, whether real or personal.

Tax—A sum of money assessed upon one's income, property and purchases, for the purpose of supporting the government.

Tax Court—A federal administrative agency which acts as a court for the purposes of determining disputes between individuals and the Internal Revenue Service.

Trial—The judicial procedure whereby disputes are determined based on the presentation of issues of law and fact. Issues of fact are decided by the trier of fact, either the judge or jury, and issues of law are decided by the judge.

Trial Court—The court of original jurisdiction over a particular matter.

Truth-In-Lending Act—A federal law which requires commercial lenders to provide applicants with detailed, accurate and understandable information relating to the cost of credit, so as to permit the borrower to make an informed decision.

Unconscionable—Refers to a bargain so one-sided as to amount to an absence of meaningful choice on the part of one of the parties, together with terms which are unreasonably favorable to the other party.

Undue Influence—The exertion of improper influence upon another for the purpose of destroying that person's free will in carrying out a particular act, such as entering into a contract.

Usurious Contract—A contract that imposes interest at a rate which exceeds the legally permissible rate.

Usury—An excessive rate of interest above the maximum permissible rate established by the state legislature.

Vitiate—To make void.

Void—Having no legal force or binding effect.

Voidable—Capable of being rendered void and unenforceable.

Voluntary Arbitration -Arbitration which occurs by mutual and free consent of the parties.

BIBLIOGRAPHY AND ADDITIONAL READING

Black's Law Dictionary, Fifth Edition. St. Paul, MN: West Publishing Company, 1979.

Cane, Michael Allen, *The Five-Minute Lawyers' Guide to Bad Debts, Credit Problems and Bankruptcy*. New York, NY: Dell Publishing Company, 1995.

Consumer Sentinel (Date Visited: September 2001) <http://www.consumer.gov/sentinel/>.

Federal Trade Commission (Date Visited: September 2001) <http://www.ftc/gov/>.

Hammond, Bob, *Life After Debt*. Franklin Lakes, NJ: Career Press, 1996.

Hibbs, Bud, *Stop It! A Consumer Guide to Effectively Stopping Collection Agency Harassment*. Fort Worth, TX: Equitable Media Services, 1992.

Hobbs, Robert, Fair Debt Collection, Third Edition. Boston, MA: National Consumer Law Center, Inc., 1996.

Internal Revenue Service (Date Visited: September 2001) <http://www.irs.ustreas.gov>.

Leonard, Robin, *Money Troubles: Legal Strategies to Cope with your Debts*. Berkeley, CA: Nolo Press., 1996.

Nickel, Gudrun M., *Debtors' Rights: A Legal Self Help Guide*. Clearwater, FL: Sphinx International, 1992.

The U.S. Postal Inspection Service (Date Visited: September 2001) <http://www.usps.gov/websites/depart/inspect>.

Warner, Ralph. Elias, Stephen, *Billpayer's Rights*. Berkeley, CA: Nolo Press, 1986.